PGCE Survival Guide

incorporating #pgcetips

Edited by Tim Handley

Illustrated by Helen Morgan

IFirst Edition
First Published August 2010

ISBN:- 978-1-4461-6490-7

For the Primary PGCE Team at UEA
...who really bring learning to life

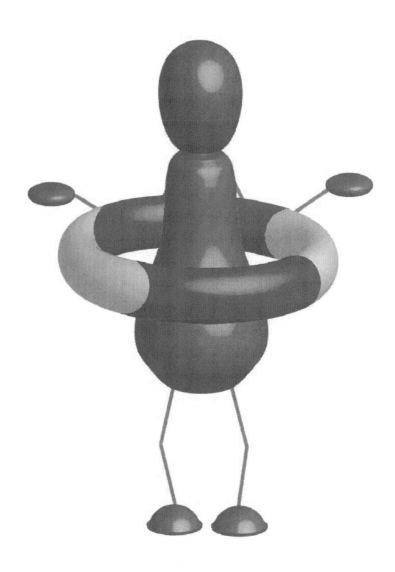

Contents

Finishing the Course 113

What we wished we'd known and our highlights 119

Final Top Tips! 123

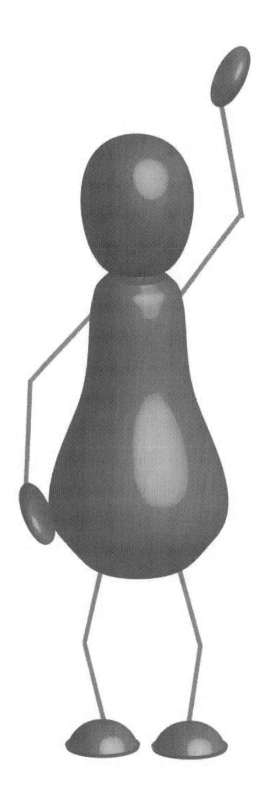

Hello!

Thanks for deciding to read the PGCE Survival Guide - a 'crowd sourced' book.

You're probably sitting there wondering what this book is all about?

Well, put simply, this book is designed to help you during your teacher training year. In it you will find information and tips for most parts of your teacher training as well as much more!

One of my best 'discoveries' during my own PGCE was the wonderful and extremely useful and helpful networks of dedicated and committed education professionals that exist online and specifically on Twitter. I soon started to build up my own PLN (Personal Learning Network) and benefited greatly from it throughout my PGCE (much more on this later in the book). When I started to put together this guide, I challenged people on Twitter to give tips to new teacher trainees by using the hashtag #pgcetips - and the response was amazing!

So splattered throughout this book you will find over 200 tips and advice from the education network on Twitter and each tip is, of course, under 140 characters!

I also discovered blogging and the amazing range of education blogs that exist. In most chapters you will also find a 'from the blogsphere' – where I have reproduced a relevant blog post (from both my own blog and others too!) that provides 'at the time' insight into the area.

I've also been lucky enough to have various different people volunteer to write sections of this book who offer their valuable insight and share their experiences.

This book is broadly aimed at anyone who is training to become a teacher. The book was originally aimed at people who are completing their PGCE, but people completing their teacher training via the myriad of other routes should also hopefully find much of the information relevant and useful (especially sections 3 and 4.) I have tried to highlight any differences between Primary and Secondary training courses throughout the book, but given my primary background the book may have a slight primary bias.

I'd love to hear your feedback on the book and you can contact me at pgcetips@classroomtales.com or contact me on Twitter @tomhenzley. My blog, www.classroomtales.com also contains all the posts that I made throughout my PGCE year.

Have a great PGCE!

Tim Handley

A word about the tweets

All the 'tweets' in the book have largely been left as they have been sent. Contractions etc have been left as they were in the original tweet. The tweets are the views and advice of the sender.

Meet The Editor

Tim Handley has just completed his Primary PGCE at the University of East Anglia in Norwich. He is just about to start his NQT year with a year 5 class at a large primary school on the East coast. Tim is passionate about the use of technology, cross curricular working and the use of images in the classroom.

He decided to write this book as he remembered the anxiety waiting for his PGCE to start and how much he wished he could find lots of firsthand experience and tips from people who had 'been there and done that' and how useful these tips could have been throughout his PGCE year.

All sections that are not attributed to someone else have been written by Tim.
Tim currently blogs at www.classroomtales.com and also blogged extensively throughout his PGCE year. Tim can be found on Twitter at @tomhenzley

Meet The Contributors

Nikki Davies has been teaching in KS2 for 6 years. She is strangely enthusiastic about assessment. As well as writing our assessment section, Nikki has taken on the large task of proof reading this book! Nikki can be found on Twitter at @knikidavies

Oliver Quinlan - Oliver Quinlan is a primary trained teacher who has just completed his NQT year with a year 4 class at Robin Hood School in Birmingham, UK. His experience in IT support in a forward thinking Early Years setting influenced a commitment to enabling children to take control of their own learning. He is a Google Certified Teacher and interested in embedding technology into the curriculum, experimenting with pedagogy, and research based approaches to teaching and learning. Oliver wrote our sections on Your Teaching Style, Doing things differently, and shared his NQT experiences in the NQT section. He can be found on Twitter @oliverquinlan and can be found online at http://www.oliverquinlan.co.uk

Mark Howell - Mark Howell, 25, is from Northampton. He is currently subject leader in Geography at a comprehensive secondary school in East Northants and teaches at KS3, GCSE and A-Level. He completed a PGCE at Plymouth University and has a degree in Geography and International Business studies from the University of Plymouth. Mark wrote our sections on Teaching for the first time and Your Mentor. He can be found on Twitter at @mark_howell101 and blogs at http://markhowell101.wordpress.com

Alan Parkinson - Alan Parkinson taught geography (& other stuff) for 20 years before joining Geog Assoc as Curric Dev Leader in 2008. He has written 3 books and been published in numerous journals & blogs at http://livinggeography.blogspot.com and can be found on Twitter at @geoblogs

Jenny Harvey - Jenny Harvey is a Mum, a wife and a third year BEd (Primary) student. Along with a passion for learning and teaching she loves finding engaging and relevant ways to integrate technology. She describes her life as chaotic but wouldn't have it any other way. Jenny contributed to our behaviour management section and can be found on Twitter at @relativism and blogs at http://relativism-studentponderings.blogspot.com

Emma Dawson - Emma Dawson is a Year 4 teacher in a rural 1-form entry Primary School in Northamptonshire. She loves trying out new technologies with her class and is interested in finding new and exciting ways to teach in a cross-curricular way. Her particular interests lie in Literacy, Languages, ICT and Gifted and Talented teaching. She wrote our section on Jobs and Applications and can be found on Twitter at @squiggle7

Gerald Haigh - Gerald Haigh was a teacher for thirty years in secondary, middle and primary schools, eleven of them as a middle school head. He's also served as a school governor and as an external examiner to teacher training courses in three HE institutions. Throughout his school career he wrote about education, mainly in the TES, and also published several books. He contributed to our behaviour management section and can be found on Twitter @gearldhaigh1

Helen Morgan - Helen trained as a secondary teacher through the Graduate Teacher Programme in Design and Technology. She currently works at the City of Stoke on Trent Sixth Form College as Course Leader Photography and Art Teacher. Her passion is for all elements of Art and Design ;jewellery, 3D, fine art, photography and graphics. She is currently developing a fully digital A'level photography course and Multimedia Graphics spin on the Art and Design Level 2 Diploma. She is committed to using modern technology to enable and engage students, allowing them to take greater responsibility for their own progress. Helen provided the illustrations for this book. She can be found on twitter @nellmog and can be found online at http://www.helenmorgan.co.uk

Amanda O'Dell - Amanda O'Dell is a Geography NQT working in East London. She trained as a teacher via the London North Consortium Graduate Training Programme at Middlesex University. Amanda wrote our section on reflective writing and can be found on twitter at @mandared

Ryan Delaney- Ryan Delaney is a third year BEd (Primary) student who decided he wanted to be a teacher the first time he stepped foot in a school at the age of five. An inspirational teacher during his final year at primary school had a huge influence in developing his interest in inclusion.

Sarah Brownsword Sarah Brownsword is a 36 year old Year 6 teacher in a Suffolk middle school, former EFL Teacher, Bookseller, HypnoBirthing Practitioner and Business Owner who retrained as a KS2 teacher at UEA in 2007. She is currently doing research for an MA in Advanced Educational Practice and lives in Norfolk with her two daughters and her fiance. Sarah wrote our section on juggling family life with the PGCE and can be found on twitter at @missbrownsword and she blogs at http://missbrownsword.blogspot.com

The Tweeters

A massive thank-you must be extended to the education community on twitter, without whom this book couldn't have happened.

After each tweet in this book you will find the username of the 'tweeter' who 'tweeted' that tweet. To find out more about them, or to follow them on twitter just go to www.twitter.com and put the username in the search box!

Twitter is a great resource to tap into during your PGCE and is a great way to start building your personal learning network (PLN). Why not sign up for a twitter account today at www.twitter.com? More information on twitter can be found on page 141.

Introduction

Congratulations!

It may be a strange way to effectively start off a book, but huge congratulations are due to you, the reader, for two reasons!

First of all, congratulations on gaining a place on your PGCE or training programme. Competition for these places is incredibly fierce, and you have shown to your training provider that you have the skills and qualities necessary to become a teacher and this is something you should remember throughout your course. You will already have shown a high level of dedication and interest and will have worked hard to get to this point - Well Done!

Secondly, congratulations on making the decision to join one of the most rewarding professions there is. I truly believe teaching is one of the best jobs in the world - you will be challenged, made to laugh, smile and have fun on a daily basis, and importantly you will play a small part in shaping the lives of the children you teach.

So have fun during your PGCE. I'm sure you will have a great year - It will be hard work (but I'm sure you've heard enough of that already!) but immensely rewarding. Enjoy every minute of it!

Originally Posted:- 01/2010
Blog Address:- classroom.com
Blogger:- Tim Handley

Why I love Teaching

I've just returned from school today and had a really positive day, the children were on task, enjoyed the lessons I taught, made real progress and I had fun! I was also told that my class teacher who I'm with is really impressed with me and the quality of my teaching- which is always good(!)

It got me thinking on the drive home about the thing I enjoy most about teaching, and why I now realise it's one of the best jobs around!

1. You get to work with lots of wonderful children, who make you smile on a daily basis.

2. You also get to work with lots of amazing 'adults' who mostly share the same passion as you! This is even more notable for me as a trainee as I get to see a selection of teachers, TA's etc...

3. The buzz you get when you see the 'lightbulb' go on is great- I witnessed this numerous times today with 'long' multiplication.

4. You have the freedom to be (relatively) creative- [as long as you stick within the curriculum]- I am particularly lucky I think to have an great class teacher/mentor in my placement school who is willing and positively encourages me to 'do different' and is prepared for it not to always work.

5.You are part of lots of young peoples development, and gain their trust- which I recognise as a real privilege.

6.You are also able to 'make a difference' to some/many of the young people you teach (corny I know but true!)

7. It doesn't necessarily feel like a 'job' and I have 'fun' (most of the time!)

8. Everyday is 'new' and different and often unpredictable!

9. You hear and learn something new every day- in fact normally many things!

So these are my reasons why I love teaching (and I've only been 'teaching' for a extremely little time) – If you're a teacher-what are yours?

TH

The PGCE Year

So you're on the PGCE - what can you expect from the year?

• You'll spend time in university - this is normally around half the course for Primary students and just under half the course for Secondary students. In university you'll cover a wide range of general things about teaching and cover subject knowledge and pedagogy

• You'll spend time on placement - each provider must give you at least 2 placements in 2 different age ranges - but your provider may structure their course on 3 (or more) shorter placements. How these placements are organized will depend on your provider, but you are likely to spend some weeks where you are both in university and school and some weeks where you are just in school.

• You'll work hard - there is no escaping it - the PGCE year is hard work. In less than a year your training provider has the task of turning you into a teacher and equipping you with the knowledge, skills and experience to teach. You will have to simultaneously manage teaching (with all it entails) along with academic work.

• It'll be fast paced.

• You will learn a lot - but more on this much later!

• It'll go quickly - despite what it may seem like at the start of your PGCE, the 8-9 months of the course will fly by and you'll soon be in June/July and qualified!

• It'll make you want to laugh and cry (and often both at the same time)
But above all - you will gain many fantastic experiences!

#pgcetips on.... The PGCE Year

Do not underestimate how bloody knackered you will be at the end of your first day. And your first week. And your first term. @Morphosaurus

DO NOT BOOK A HOLIDAY for October Half Term - you'll just want to sleep this time round! @smckane

The year will fly by but make sure you stop occasionally to think about how much you're enjoying it and how much you've learned! @Mandared

Like your school days you probably won't appreciate how much fun the course is until it's over Remember to stop & enjoy periodically @relativism

It might feel like a year to survive but IS a year to enjoy learn network and lay good foundations for your career @stevewn

Accept that your PGCE will become your life for a while. It's all consuming but worth it. @Cl aireLotriet

Enjoy yourself! You are going to be in a job where you are surrounded by enthusiastic open minds and no two days are the same. @ClaireLotriet

Juggling PGCE with family life.
By Sarah Brownsword

Embarking on a PGCE is a full on, full time, hard working experience for everyone but even more so if you're not a recent graduate and have your own family commitments to juggle at the same time as studying. When I did my Primary PGCE 3 years ago I was a single parent to two children under 7 and these are my tips for surviving the PGCE.

Be organised but not hard on yourself

It's important to think ahead and do things like plan meals, schedule family time and not leave planning or assignments to the last minute, but at the same time you're not a super hero and it's ok to let standards slip.

You can't do everything yourself, prioritise and delegate.

If help is there by way of family or friends – use it!

I worked when the children were in bed, never before, ensuring they had the attention they needed and so did my PGCE.

Get childcare sorted early, my child minder was a god send.

Money

If you've given up work to study money can be tight during the PGCE year but help is available for parents in the form of childcare grants, single parent grants and bursaries. Most universities have hardship funds or loans, don't be afraid to ask for these it's what the money is there for. As a student parent my children were eligible for free school meals which not only saved me a lot of money but also time, knowing they had had a hot meal at lunch time saved me cooking every night.

You don't need to reinvent the wheel

It's a cliché but it's true, I listened to many of my PGCE colleagues tell of the hours they spent designing resources whereas I spent minutes downloading something just as good from the internet! Search online first, chances are you will find what you need or better.

Believe in yourself

I did my PGCE more than ten years after I originally graduated, writing an essay after all that time is a daunting task, but you can do it! Give yourself plenty of time and ask for help from tutors if you need it.

Your Strengths

As a parent I found that in many ways I was already 'ahead' in the PGCE game right from the start, many trainees actually have very little experience with children. As a parent you will already 'get' children, you know what children of certain ages look like, think like, play like and talk like, other trainees will have to learn this. You will be more confident in organising and managing children's behaviour and have the ability to tell whether a child is really sick or not that only comes with parenting!

Enjoy and relax!

It's hard work but it was one of the most enjoyable years I've had. Take time to relax and spend with your family - I worked late every night but weekends were for my children, it was making that time that made it easier to endure the difficult bits.

Your First Day on the Course

You've spent all summer agonising over the pre-course information.

You've read copious amounts.

You've spent ages wondering about the hectic year that you know you have ahead of you.

It seems like you have been preparing and waiting for this moment for ever.

But the time has come, and you approach the first day on the course. You may have a sleepless night. You feel a mixture of excitement and nerves (for that's only natural!). You wonder if the first day will mark the end of your life as you know it (probably not!) and you wonder who you'll meet and if they'll be like you (probably!).

Your first day on the PGCE should also be a cause for celebration - you have made it! You have competed against thousands of people for a place and you have been selected.

Two things will probably characterise your first day - Queues and new people!

You will spend what will seem like an age queuing up for things. Whether that's to find out where your first lecture is, to join a union(s) and pick up lots of free goodies, to register, to get your university card , to arrange a parking permit or for countless other things! Sadly you have to put up with these queues – one of the main functions of your first day is to make sure you are set up for the year ahead with everything at the university - something that is important considering the fast pace of the year. Bear in mind that PGCE courses usually start 3 or 4 weeks before usual undergraduate courses – on one hand, this means that the central university departments (IT, Library, Car Parking, finance etc) may not have got everything into gear for everyone on the PGCE, but on the other it also means that if anything isn't sorted properly the central departments will have very few other students to sort out - so by the end of your first week you should be all set university wise!

It also goes without saying that you will meet lots of new people - both your fellow students and your university tutors. Try to speak with as many people as you can - but don't worry if you don't speak to someone 'important' - you will get to know a lot of the people you meet on your first day very well over the next year!

The exact format of your first day will obviously vary depending on your training provider and you probably won't know what to expect until the day! But it will usually look something like this:-

-Some form of introductory lecture(s) - you will be introduced to the PGCE probably by the course director or somebody else senior within the department - you'll be told how great you are (as you've been selected) and perhaps given a bit of an insight into the year ahead.

-You'll then probably get split off into some form of groups. This will normally be the group that you will spend time doing your 'Professional studies' elements of your university programme with (but again this varies widely) and will probably cross phase (so have people from every strand of the Primary PGCE programme in) - think of this group like it is your tutor group at high school! You will meet your professional development tutor - this is the person who will be your first port of call on the course and whose primary responsibility it is to support you and make sure everything is ok! You'll then probably spend some time in this group getting to know each other and dealing with admin tasks (you'll probably also be given a lot of paper!)

-You'll also have to do the aforementioned queuing! You'll probably get the chance to meet reps from all the main teaching unions who will promptly bestow lots of bags full of freebies - expect to come away with at least 2 diaries, wall planners, memory sticks and whistles! They will also offer you free membership for your PGCE year (more on that below!)

-You'll also probably be given a course handbook which explains all the administrative and practical sides of the course (whilst it may be boring reading - it's recommended you read it so you know all the info in case you need it!) as well as things like the timetable etc!
Your first day will probably be exhausting, but will hopefully really get you excited about the amazing year ahead! The hard work will probably start tomorrow (as there's so much to fit in!) - so get another good nights sleep and be ready for the start of the PGCE course 'proper'.

Here are some tips for your first day:-

Join a Union! As mentioned above, all the main unions offer free membership for trainee students - so most people end up joining all of them! Joining a union is considered by most to be vital when working in schools - hopefully you'll never need the services they provide, but it's useful to know that you have legal and practical support there if you need it!

Speak to people! As scary as it is, don't be tempted to be withdrawn - make a proactive effort to talk to people (but don't appear crazy!)

Try to remember names! You'll meet lots of people - but try to remember some of the names of your fellow students - especially those in your teaching or professional development group.

Sort out all the practicalities! E-mail addresses, logins, library/campus cards etc! Make sure they are sorted now so they don't have to be later when you are busy.

Do your paperwork! Make sure you have filled in all the paperwork that you need to! Especially make sure you have completed your bursary form so you can receive your first month of your training bursary on time!

Get Contacts! Make sure you have contact details for your tutor and anybody else who is likely to be important to you - and keep these in a safe place!

Some general #pgcetips

Don't expect anybody who is not doing the PGCE to understand how you are feeling. Use your fellow students to unload!
@shellbelle21

"Waterloo Road"" is not realistic portrayal of school life. ""Teachers"" is. Suggest acquisition of the box set." ## @morphosaurus

join twitter - build a network of fellow students & teachers. They have taught me so much, sometimes I'm even able to give back
@relativism

Drink less than you did at University.
@Frogphilip

University

Your first experience of life on your PGCE is likely to be university based, and time spent in university will make up around half of your training year.

But what is expected of you? What exactly can you expect in university sessions? How do you cope with the demands of assignments? Read on to find out!

University - what is it all about?

You will probably spend around half your time (less for secondary) on your PGCE in university. So what should you expect?

Your university sessions will primarily contain two things: - Subject Knowledge and Professional Studies/Development sessions.

Subject Knowledge sessions essentially do what they say on the tin - they aim to equip you with (some) of the subject knowledge you need to teach and some of the pedagogical approaches to teaching the subject.

Professional Studies/Development sessions can be seen as a catch all for everything else - in these sessions the focus is on the professional skills you need as a teacher.

On days you are in university you can probably expect to have sessions between 9-5 (with a lunch break) on most days. The exact ways universities structure their days vary greatly and will be different for primary and secondary students – you will of course find out how your provider structures your time within the first few days of the course.

You will be told that attendance is vital - and really it is! You are expected to attend ALL university sessions and a register will probably be taken. Any absence will be recorded and may be reported in your attendance figure in any reference your provider gives you. Good attendance also is essential as it forms part of one of the QTS standards (more on those later) which you have to meet. Whilst you may not see the immediate relevance of a session, more often than not these will be useful to you either later in the course or in your teaching career.

That being said - universities will of course allow you time off if you need it! But as a rule you should treat attending university sessions like you would treat attending a full time job.

On the whole university sessions are enjoyable, useful and often inspiring! They provide a (sometimes unwanted) break from placement and equip you with the skills and knowledge that you need to be successful. You will also spend time with your fellow trainees - something which you will probably come to cherish and miss whilst on placement - enjoy your time in university whilst it lasts!

QTS, PGCE and all that...

You will probably have heard a lot of mention of QTS, and if you haven't heard of it by now, you certainly will hear it mentioned a lot during your training!

QTS stands for Qualified Teacher Status and it's what you need to teach in any maintained state school or non-maintained specialist school in England and Wales. In other words it is the essential thing that you are aiming to get at the end of your teacher training. You can get QTS through numerous routes - the PGCE just being one of them.

In order to achieve QTS you must prove you meet a set of standards (called Q standards) - you will be given them in various forms at the start of the course, but they can also be found at http://www.tda.gov.uk/partners/ittstandards/guidance_08/qts.aspx. These are the first set of standards you will have to meet in your teaching career - there are further sets (C standards for Core standards which you have to meet to pass your NQT induction, P standards if you want to go onto the upper pay scale and so on). The standards cover all areas of your role as a teacher - from relationships with adults, to your professional conduct and your planning, teaching and classroom management and it is your training provider who 'recommends' you for the award of QTS.

You will come to know the standards well, and your training provider will have their own way in which they want you to evidence your progress towards the standards (some require portfolios of evidence, others base it mainly on observations and your own evaluations - it varies widely!). But don't let the standards rule your life - they are things that you will naturally meet in the process of learning to become an effective teacher.

Whilst we are on the subject of qualifications it's also worth mentioning the PGCE itself. Just to be confusing a 'PGCE' can normally stand for one of two things:-

A PostGraduate Certificate in Education - this is taught and assessed at masters level (i.e. postgraduate) and will include some credits (usually 60 - a third) towards a masters degree.

A Professional Graduate Certificate in Education - this is taught and assessed at the level of a third year undergraduate - you won't receive any credits towards a masters degree.

Both forms of PGCE will also lead to QTS. Your training provider will let you know which one they offer - as a rule of thumb if you are training at a university you are likely to be able to take the PostGraduate Certificate in Education although some universities also offer the Professional Graduate programme. The difference between the two is normally minimal - you still have to do the same assignments but the level at which they need to be written varies (it needs to be at masters level for the postgraduate but undergraduate level for the professional graduate). The level at which your practical teaching is assessed remains the same.

It's important to say that you don't need a PGCE to teach in the UK - all that is required is that you have QTS.

Subject Sessions and Subject Knowledge

A significant amount of time that you spend at university on the Primary PGCE (secondary PGCErs have less subject sessions due to already being a specialist in their subject!) will be in 'subject' or 'curriculum' sessions. This section is therefore more directly relevant to Primary PGCE students than those on secondary programmes.

The aim of the curriculum sessions are to provide some input in relation to the subject knowledge you need to teach and some of the pedagogical approaches which you can use to teach the subject.

Remember as a primary teacher, you need to be able to teach all of the subjects taught at primary level. You may not have done some of these subjects since you were 13! But fear not - the subject sessions provided by your training provider will be designed to allow you to pick it all up again quickly. People often have anxieties about certain subjects (maths being a common one!) but your tutors are used to dealing with these and will generally approach everything 'from the beginning', and by the end of the course you will hopefully end up feeling more confident in your ability to teach all subjects!

The subjects taught at primary level are split into 3 categories:-

Core Subjects - these are Maths, English and Science
Foundation Subjects - Art and Design, Music, History, Design and Technology, Geography, Physical Education, ICT, and Modern Foreign Languages (MFL)

Other Statutory Subjects: - PSHCE (Personal, Social, Health and Citizenship Education) and Religious Education (which follows a locally agreed syllabus for each local authority)

You will generally receive more hours of core subject sessions and ICT and generally the same amount of hours for each foundation and statutory subject.

People often comment how having a curriculum/subject day at university makes them feel like they are back at secondary school (in a good way!) - as you will probably find yourself moving around from Maths to English to Art etc!

Curriculum sessions can take many forms, but they will often involve a university tutor teaching a session to you, like they would to a primary class (albeit normally more condensed and at a higher pace!) - this is great as it enables you to experience different teaching styles and pedagogical approaches first hand - it also means that you will generally get to have 'fun' and to have a go at lots of practical things (especially in Art and PE - they aren't kidding when they tell you the PGCE is a highly participatory course - expect to do a lot of things you haven't done for ages!).

One of the many advantages of subject sessions is they often give you ideas that you can use and adapt in your own teaching!

Curriculum sessions may also include some direct teaching and exploration around the different approaches you can take to the subject or topic area.

Curriculum sessions won't, however, cover everything that you could possibly be required to teach - as this is simply impossible in the time allowed. You will find yourself needing to research and teach yourself different areas (especially in the foundation subjects) when you are required to teach them - but this will be a normal occurrence throughout your career. You will be able to apply the pedagogical approaches that you pick up from your subject sessions to most topics in the subject concerned!

Originally Posted:-20/02/2010
Blog Address:- classroomtales.com
Blogger:- Tim Handley

Back at School

This week was a 'curriculum week' for us on the PGCE- that meant that we basically swapped teaching for being taught...

On curriculum weeks, we spend the time being 'taught' ourselves. I can't help feeling it is a lot like being back in school- we start at 9am with a whole cohort lecture, and then have 3 subjects for 2 hours each. We move down the corridors to science labs, art rooms, maths classrooms, get changed for PE, etc and all congregate in groups at lunchtime etc- as I say a lot like being in secondary school!

As with any PGCE, we obviously receive differing amount of input per subject- the core subjects (Maths, Eng, Science plus ICT) have the most and the foundation (pretty much everything else) get about 12 hours of input over the course. One of the things I think is great about the my PGCE provider is they do ensure we have input on all the subjects, including History, Geography, R.E and PSHCE- which apparently isn't the case everywhere.

In the sessions, we are basically taught some of the curriculum content (all be it very condensed- which is obvously needed!) and also sometimes focus on how to teach/plan the subject etc... The sessions are often very practical/participatory and we often are given and take part in the same activities that we could give/use in our own teaching- for instance in D+T this week we made sandwiches, in English made a radio programme, in Science took part in 'crime scene' investigations and in P.E had a 'go' on the large apparatus.

Last term, cirrocumulus weeks were the 'norm' so we looked forward to them, and also built up great relationships with our fellow trainees in our teaching groups (we have both teaching groups- made up of people with the same age specialism (i.e. KS2 for me) and Professional Development Groups- which are cross specialism).

But this week, it all felt rather strange- and I know this was a feeling shared by lots of us on the course. Lots of people were very disgruntled. On the Monday, if I had got a pound for every time I heard 'I'd just rather be in school' I'd have a lot of money!

I guess this is because we aren't as used to them this term, and we are getting increasingly used to being infront of the class, rather than being in the class. It is only natural for us to feel that we'd rather be in school, as I personally learn so much for being in school, teaching, and it is what we are getting used to. I guess it's taking us out of what is increasingly feeling more normal to us. But of course, university input is also valuable, and I obviously see the need for curriculum weeks!

The course tutors know this- and I do think the course is designed well in this respect- we had the bulk of our curriculum input last term, which gave us a good grounding in all the subjects, and now we can spend the majority of our time in schools, getting 'practice'!

I know lots of people on the course don't feel they learn a great deal on the curriculum weeks- but I've been reflecting on this and think this is because it is a different type of learning that takes place.

Whilst we are in schools we learn/experience the day to day practical things which impact, often immediately on our own teaching- we therefore quickly see the application of what we have learnt/experienced in other words a lot of the learning is experiential.

But on curriculum weeks, we are shown techniques, and given/refreshed on subject knowledge that has no **immediate** use to us- I think it is often difficult to see the direct impact of what we are taught in curriculum weeks to us as teachers as we, naturally, won't always have an application for it **straight away** which gives some people the feeling of learning for learning's sake that a lot of people comment on feeling.

I've heard numerous times from people on the course that they have 'never used anything they've been taught in university'. It's seems rather 'expected' to me that I can only name two occasions where I have directly used/adapted a session/activity we were given in university- afterall we are not all going to be teaching the same things as we are being taught in university etc!

We are not being trained to be robots and regurgitate sessions/adaptations of sessions that have been given to us- we are being trained to be **reflective teachers** who use their judgement and 'skill' to teach in a way that matches the **individual needs of the children we teach.**

But... I know a lot of the ways I have approached topics/subjects/my general teaching have their grounding in the sessions we have experienced in university.

Just as a few examples I have taught my science lessons in a variety of different ways including numerous adaptations of the exploration/pupil led methods which have been demonstrated to us in science sessions at university, I have used ideas and principles from our Drama sessions in the teaching of a wide variety of subjects, and have applied techniques that were shown to us during a RE session when teaching science.

Personally without the experience of the curriculum weeks, I feel I wouldn't feel anywhere near as confident (not that I feel really confident but...) as I do now, and I certainly wouldn't be able to approach planning whole units of work etc...

Whilst we are taught the sessions in the most part like we are children (all be it talked to like adults) if people only take out of it what you would do if you were a child, then in my opinion people are rather missing the point!

It is up to **us** to make the most out of the experiences we are given, **critically reflect** on them and apply what we have learnt from these reflections to our own teaching and build up an increasing toolkit of teaching strategies etc...

So I don't think the university can 'do' anything to change peoples perceptions of curriculum weeks at this stage in the course. Afterall, it's up to us, as adults, to make the most of the amazing experiences we are given.

One really positive thing that everyone has mentioned this week is how great it is to be back in our teaching groups! It can sometimes seem a bit 'lonely' out in schools (I guess even more so if you don't live with other student teachers!) and it's been really great to re-connect, share experiences and generally catchup.

Afterall I'm sure these groups will form the start of our professional network, and I also know I will gain
some valuable friendships from them too!

As always I'd be interested to hear your thoughts!
TH

Professional Development and Professional Studies

As well as the subject sessions discussed in the previous section, you will also have Professional Development/Studies sessions during your time at university.

These sessions focus on the 'general' professional skills that you need to become an effective teacher. These are skills that you will be able to apply across subjects and/or age ranges and will usually be delivered in a cross age range (for primary) or cross subject (for secondary) groups - make the most of this chance to spend time with people who are focusing on a different age range or subject than you!

The content of these sessions is wide, but you can expect to cover things like:-

- How children learn
- Children's lives outside the classroom
- Techniques for observing - both children and other teachers teaching.
- Parents and other partners in a child's education
- Classroom organisation/management
- Behaviour management
- Equality, Diversity and Inclusion
- Learning outside the classroom and educational trips
- Planning
- Assessment
- Report Writing
- Job Hunting and interviews
- And much more!

The sessions will be planned by your training provider to support your progression on placements and you may find that you have a particular focus for a week which you will back up by focused observations and tasks during your time in school. Like curriculum sessions, professional studies sessions will be delivered in a variety of styles, but you are more likely to meet traditional lecturing and seminar style activities and outside speakers in your professional studies sessions than you are in your curriculum sessions.

Your training provider could spend 15+ hours lecturing on behaviour management (or any other area for that matter) but this would not make up for time spent observing practising teachers teaching and teaching yourself in schools - as this is where your 'real' learning will take place and this is why you are likely to have only a couple of hours input in each area. You will probably feel that you haven't had enough input in X (behaviour management, planning and assessment being common areas!) or that the input for Y didn't come soon enough in the course. It is best to approach these sessions as a valuable introduction – your learning and development in these areas will take place on placement when you are observing and teaching. After all, everybody's experience on placement is different and you will need to develop strategies and skills that meet the needs of your placement class(es). You will learn an incredible amount from your class teacher/mentor and your experience in schools.

Directed Time and Giving yourself a break!

During the PGCE you will usually hear that you have X number of hours of 'directed time' for each subject or element of the course. This is basically an indication to the number of hours that you are expected to put into the course outside of taught sessions and placements.

You should take the stated number of hours as a guide - ultimately you need to spend the number of hours that you need to and this could be more or less than the hours set out by your training provider. You should expect, however, to spend a significant portion of your 'free' time doing things for the PGCE, especially during the first term (this gets replaced by planning, assessment etc when you are on placement.) If you are lucky you may also be given some 'study days' during the year for you to carry out some of your directed time activities.

The things you will find you need to do during directed time varies widely - and will probably include reading, note taking, doing exercises (especially in maths and English), preparation for your subject audits and research and observations for your assignments.

Use your directed time wisely - if you have a lull and don't have much to do, look ahead and try to make a start on something that you know is coming up like an assignment or audit - you will be grateful of it when the time comes and you are busy with placement etc!

That being said, it is essential that you make sure you do give yourself a break - it is very tempting to spend ALL of your time on things that are related to the PGCE - but if you do this you will probably find yourself burning out. Make sure you put aside some time - perhaps an evening and one day at the weekend a week in which you will not do anything to do with the PGCE (including talking about it!) - and be strict with yourself and stick to it wherever possible!

Assignments...

Like it or loathe it, you are probably going to have to write numerous assignments, essays or studies during your teacher training. The advice in this section aims to try to minimise the pain from having to write the assignments!

One of the main tips may seem obvious yet is rarely listened to (by myself included!) Start your assignments as early as possible and don't leave it until the last minute. Try to plan ahead - realistically you will probably find you won't be able to get much done on assignments when your teaching commitment has picked up on placement (you'll be busy planning etc!) so try to make a good start on assignments prior to placement blocks if at all possible. It is tempting to leave everything to the last minute - especially considering how busy your training year will be - but this will only cause more stress and many sleepless nights in the long run - which isn't good for anyone - especially if you are meant to be teaching!

But apart from this, what else can you do to minimise the stress that can be caused by assignments?

First of all, it's important that you understand the level at which you are required to write the assignment at and the style it has to take. This will largely depend on your training provider and which type of course you are following. If you are doing a Postgraduate Certificate in Education then the assignments will have to be written at 'masters level'. If you are doing a Professional Graduate Certificate in education, GTP or SCITT than your assignments are likely to have to be written at the level of an undergraduate essay.

It is also vital that you find out and make sure you understand the criteria against which you will be assessed before you start researching and writing your assignment. All your assignments will be assessed against selected QTS standards and if you are doing a masters level course you will also have a separate set of M-Level criteria to meet as well - QTS and M-level criteria are not normally dependant on each other - in other words you can achieve QTS in an essay without achieving M-Level and vice versa. Your training provider should make the criteria clear to you, but if they have not or if you have any questions make sure you ask them!

Your training provider should provide you with a list of assignments and submission dates at the start of the course. If you are not given this, try to find out as soon as possible what you will be required to hand in and when you are required to do it by. Make sure you mark these dates on numerous calendars and wall planners as it will be your responsibility to make sure you start work on them and that they are handed in by the deadline.

It may be some time ago that you have last written an academic piece of writing - but don't worry! Remember that lots of people will be in the same position as you - even those who have recently completed a degree may well find that the style of writing required on your course is very different to that which they had to produce previously. Your training provider will normally offer you sessions on how to write at the level that they require and lots of advice and tips can be found by searching the internet.

You will need to ensure that you reference your work correctly so that you do not get accused of plagiarism! Most education departments will require a variation on the Harvard referencing system (a great guide on referencing using the Harvard system can be found at http://libweb.anglia.ac.uk/referencing/harvard.htm) but it is vital you make sure you understand the reference system required by your training provider - as they may have adapted the system or have their own requirements. In order to make your referencing easy, make sure you note down where you have got information, quotations or ideas from when you are note making - there is nothing worse than not being able to work out where something has come from!

You will probably find that 'physical' books will be in short supply in the library which you have access to - this is almost bound to happen when you consider the number of trainees vs the number of books! There is little you can effectively do about this - if you want to use lots of physical books, try to get to the library and get books out as soon as you know what could be useful for a particular assignment. If a book is out of the library but you think it will be useful then make sure you request it - even if you think there is little chance you will get the book, libraries do look at the number of requests when considering which books to order.

So with the availability of books probably limited, you will find yourself turning to the wealth of material online - in journals, association magazines, websites, e-books and the like. This is great as you will probably find much more information online than you would in a book - and it is likely to be more up to date too. This being said, you should try to include material from books and journals/online sources wherever possible.

Whilst the availability of online material is great, it can be rather daunting - simply because there is so much of it! It can often be difficult to track down the exact information you need - but here are some tips and useful website to help you:-

•Be precise in your searches and narrow them down as much as possible. You can start narrow and widen out your criteria if you are not finding the information you need.
•Make sure you include education (or similar) in your search if you find you are picking up lots of medical (or another subject) articles and journals. It is also often helpful to use the OR operator – for instance to search for Primary OR Elementary so that you can pick up articles written on both sides of the Atlantic.
•Use google scholar - scholar.google.com – to search for articles. You can even tell it which university you belong to (just click on preferences) and it will try to tell you exactly where you can access the article and also often search your university library catalogue. The 'cited by' link on Google scholar searches can also be really useful - click on it to see who has cited the article/book and you may find some other relevant articles. You can also restrict searches to specific years or authors etc.
•Don't underestimate the usefulness of abstracts - abstracts should provide a good summary of the article which will help you determine if it is worth reading in full. Sometimes all you will be able to access is an abstract of the article - if you can't track down access to the full article then using the abstract itself may still be useful.

•Make sure you are signed into Athens (if you are provided access to it) before you search - Athens is an authentication system for universities which enables you to access lots of different journal databases for free. If you are logged in before you search it will make accessing articles easier, and make sure you look for the 'log in using Athens' if a journal website asks you to login or pay!

•The teacher training resource bank is amazing (www.ttrb.ac.uk) – it contains reviews of lots of articles, papers and government journals and will give you very concise information about why it's important and who it may be useful to etc. It also has an e-librarian service which will help you track down relevant articles (but normally searching their previous answers will help you - saving having to ask yourself!). Make sure you search on the ttrb – you'll be surprised what you can find!

•The British Education Index http://www.leeds.ac.uk/bei/index.html is also really helpful and has lots of free to access material - it is well worth searching here as it restricts your search to education journals etc.

•If you can't access a book in physical form, see if it is available on books.google.com – you will often find that the book or excerpts from it are available to view for free online.

•Your university or training provider will almost certainly have their own system in which you can search for relevant articles - try experimenting with this and seeing if you can get training on how to use it effectively.

Once you have written the assignment-

•Make sure you proofread it well! The last thing you want is for language/grammar errors to be picked up!

•If possible get someone else to proofread it for you as well.

•Make sure you haven't gone over the word count!

•Check that all your appendices and reference lists are in place and correctly formatted.

•Avoid the temptation to read other people's work on the course, especially if it is near the deadline - people approach assignments in different ways and most of them are acceptable! You don't want to cause yourself panic if you find out that someone else has approached it in a different way to you!

•Present it well - make sure it is fastened together, avoid putting each page in a plastic wallet (makes it a pain to mark) and try to present it in some form of folder or binding.

•Hand it in - and try to take the next night off!

You will probably face a substantial wait before you get your assignment back - when you do, make sure you read the feedback (both positive and negative) well and take it on board so you can improve your next assignment. If you do happen to fail any part of the assignment - don't worry! Your provider will probably provide you with various opportunities to re-work the assignments and they will offer you support so you can achieve all the criteria.

The final thing to say about assignments is to try to see the relevance to your day to day teaching. Assignments are designed to help you develop as a teacher and to reflect on how children learn, your professional practice and the theory that underpins teaching - if you approach it from this angle, rather than assignments being just another pointless thing required by your training provider, you are far less likely to find them as stressful!

#pgcetips on.... Assignments

Reference articles from ed journals like the ASE publications which have content relevant to the topic of your assignment @asober

Remember to draw upon and refer to personal experiences both in and out of school. @Daviderogers

Don't leave your uni assignments until the night before!!!!! @shellbelle21

Some people will not agree with your views on education accept that and focus on what you believe in.@MultiMartin

Hard thing for a scientist is remembering - you must write as a social scientist in all your essays - write about shades of grey @smckane

Writing reflectively and not an English teacher? Think how your mum would phrase it; never forget the good as well as the bad @smckane

keep a scrapbook of the little notes that the pupils give you as they can help get you through an assignment with a smile @relativism

Don't wait till a week before deadline before starting coursework. Reading you have to do for this is useful in your teaching too @Caro_lann

Audits and Skills Tests

In order to achieve QTS you have to pass 3 QTS skills tests - in Maths, English and ICT. These tests are designed to assess your 'functional' skills in these areas - and the same tests are taken by ALL teacher training students - regardless of if they are training to teach primary or secondary and/or what subject they are specialising in. You need to register on the TDA's skills tests website (http://www.tda.gov.uk/skillstests.aspx) shortly after the start of the course.

The tests are free to take, you can take them at any point during the year and they are administered by Pearson - the same people who deal with the driving theory tests. You can take the tests as many times as you need to pass, but you must pass all 3 tests before your training provider can recommend you for QTS.

Most people think it is best to get the tests out of the way as soon as possible so they don't interfere with your main placements; the Christmas holidays are usually a popular time to take the tests!

Practice tests are available online and it is well worth trying them out beforehand to see how you do and to get used to the format. Some people decide to do the practice tests and then go ahead and do the real things without any revision and see how they do (and then concentrate on any test they have failed) and other prefer to revise thoroughly - it's completely up to you - you need to do what you feel most comfortable with.

The main thing to say about the QTS tests is don't panic - most people do not find them as scary as they are made out to be! If you are struggling with any aspect of the tests ask for help from your training provider - they will normally be only too pleased to give it you!

Subject Audits

As well as the QTS tests, there is a requirement in the QTS standards that you show that you:-

> *"Have a secure knowledge and understanding of their subjects/curriculum areas and related pedagogy to enable them to teach effectively across the age and ability range for which they are trained. (Q14)"*

If you are doing a Primary PGCE, this means all subjects, but usually with a focus on Maths, English, Science and ICT. In order to provide evidence for these standards most training providers will carry out some form of subject audit in these subjects. This is a supportive process designed to help you fill in any gaps in your subject knowledge. The form of these audits varies widely - it could be a traditional test, a questionnaire, a portfolio or something else – but what is important to bear in mind is that the purpose is to support you - not to test you for the sake of it.   Again, don't panic about the audits - if areas for development are identified this should be viewed as a positive thing as the support you need will be offered to you. It's also important to bear in mind that throughout the PGCE you will receive subject sessions on all areas of the curriculum - also bear in mind that you are not expected to be at degree (or A-level, or even GCSE) standard in these subjects - just at a standard which enables you to teach the subjects effectively at primary level!

Placements and Teaching

You probably can't wait to get on placement, to get 'stuck in' and see some great practice and experience teaching first hand - after all, it's what you're training to do!
But it's also natural to feel pretty anxious and nervous. It can seem like there is a lot riding on you and an awful lot to learn.

In this section all the key elements of your placements will be covered and lots of hints and tips will be given - from what to do when you find out your placement to how to cope with observations and assessments.

Sit tight and enjoy the ride through the crazy world of placements!

Finding Out Your Placement

One of the things you will be anxious to find out when you start the course is where you will be for your first school placement. It is only natural that you will be keen to find out this piece of vital information - after all, you will be spending a considerable amount of time at the school over the coming months.

But – you may not find out anything about your placement school until a couple of weeks into the course. Organising placements is an incredibly complex task for providers and they will need to confirm the number of students actually enrolled on the course and also check with the schools at the start of term that they are still happy to have students (as circumstances often change in schools). The last thing you want is to be given a placement and have it changed at the last minute (although that may still happen occasionally!) Even though I know it may not seem like it at the time, your provider will make sure you know your placement information as soon as they can.

But when you do find out your placement school, what should you do?

•**Not hold any negative images or preconceptions of the school.** If you know the area and have heard rumours about the school (good or bad) remember they are only that - rumours. A school that has a 'bad' reputation can still be a wonderful placement. Remember your training provider would not send trainees to the school if they were not confident you would get a high quality training experience there. Equally, don't give anybody else a negative view of their placement school.

•**Don't try to change it**! Unless there is any really valid reason why you shouldn't be placed at the school.

•**Google map it!** Find out where it is! Bear in mind that your placement could be a considerable distance away - hour commutes each way are not unknown, especially in rural areas. Likewise if you don't have a car, bear in mind that you may need to catch multiple buses to get to your school. You may think "but 'x' school is closer" or realise that you will be driving past 15 primary schools on route to your placement school, but remember that your provider has to find placements for everybody and will try to make the distances people have to travel as fair as possible - remember also that not all schools in an area will have students. Your provider will have placed you as close as they can. Whilst we are on the subject of google maps, having a look at the school on google earth can also be useful!

•**Find the school website**. Most schools will have a website - find it! (If you can't, try schoolname.authorityname.sch.uk which may work!) Read it, see what you can pick up from the website, but be careful not to form any negative preconceptions about the school. You can often work out a lot from a website with a bit of detective work - the staff list for instance will give you an idea how many teachers and teaching assistants there are, and the class names/pages will tell you how many classes there are in a year and how the school is structured etc. If you can find a copy of the school brochure on the website, read it! If the school publishes newsletters online, read the most recent ones - it'll give you a good idea of what's going on in the school currently!

•**Don't read the OFSTED report** - now I know this one seems counter-intuitive - after all, shouldn't you be finding out as much information as possible before your arrive? Some people will suggest reading the report, but I personally believe (as do a lot of people) that reading the schools OFSTED report is not recommended. Here's why:-

You can't change your placement.

Reading the OFSTED report may colour your initial reaction and view of the school - it is best to make up your own mind, once you have actually spent some time in the s school.

OFTSED reports can often be 2-3 years old - schools can change a lot in this time!

Areas for improvement on OFSTED reports will probably have improved or be a prior-ity for the school - so will not be that relevant to you anyway!

A school's OFSTED report does not dictate what the placement will be like - schools with poor OFSTED reports can be fantastic placement schools - just like those with excellent ones can!

If you read something that you perceived to be 'bad' you would be worrying about it until you got to the school - it's not worth the worry!

You can't change the placement - yes I know I've already said this one but it's the main reason why you shouldn't read the report!

But having said that - it can be helpful to read the report a few days into your placement - when you have had the opportunity to make your own judgements about the school.

Who is placed where will probably be the 'hot topic' on the course for a few days!

Fast forward a few weeks...

Before you even get to your first day of placement, you should usually make contact with your placement school. Your training provider will tell you when you can do this from, but it's usually advisable to make contact with your school at least a week before your first scheduled placement day. If you are at a school with multiple trainees on placement your training provider may ask only one person to make contact on behalf of the group - if this is the case make sure you know who this is and that you find out all the information from them!

Try to avoid calling the school at what are traditionally 'busy' times for the school office - that is the periods around the start and end of school and the start of lunchtime - you are likely to get a much better response when the office isn't trying to deal with 10 parents at once!

Don't necessarily expect to speak to the head, deputy or a teacher in the school - the school receptionist will probably know all the information and will probably be expecting your call - and as you will learn very quickly, office staff generally know everything! Sometimes the office staff will ask you to speak to X – and that is obviously great too, but don't be put off if you don't speak to a member of teaching staff on your first call. When you call you should obviously introduce yourself, explain that you are a trainee teacher at X university/course and that you are looking forward to starting your placement with the school on the Y. Explain you are phoning to confirm arrangements for the first placement day.

When you contact the school try to find out:-
• What time they need you at school by on your first day
• Where you should go and who you should ask for
• What the parking arrangements are (make sure you can access the school car park if needed - many schools have barriers, gates etc which require a code or key)
• What time the school day runs to and from (if you can't find this out on the websites
• Whether there are any special events, visits etc on your first day.

If there is anything that doesn't seem right when you phone the school, let your training provider know. It is not unknown, for example, for trainees to phone up schools and it be the first the school knows (or remembers!) of them having a student - and it is much better to sort this out beforehand than to turn up completely out of the blue!

Try not to over-analyse this call! Some people will come off the phone armed with a huge bank of information - who they are placed with, their teacher's name, the year group, special needs in the class, school dinner arrangements - I even know one trainee who was given the names of the school's pets! But don't expect this level of information - you will find this out on your first day, and as nice as it would probably be to know it beforehand, you don't need to know it. Schools may be still sorting out the fine details of your placement - so if you are not given this information, don't let it put you off or form any impression about the school.

Now get ready to enjoy your first experience teaching in school!

#pgcetips on.... What to do before placement

Read the #movemeon book @chris_1974 [http://movemeon.wikispaces.com/]

Get yourself a professional email account from Google and unlock all the apps they offer (free) keep your social email separate!
@didactylos

Don't read OFSTED report but at some point talk to mentor about it he'll be able to talk context to it.   @chris_1974

You're making the transition from student to teacher. Make sure you lock down your facebook account. Set pics to friends only :) @dannynic

....and get grown up email address no dodgy embarrassing teen stuff @andyjb

This is a year to be a student and to become a teacher: take an active part in both communities. @Mberry

Get on Twitter and follow useful people! @siennaev

Your First Day on Placement

So the day has come. You're about to head off to a school - it could be round the corner, or it could be miles away, but it is going to be your 'home' for the next period of your training. A mixture of feelings are probably running through your body - nerves, excitement, anticipation, worry and many more too!

So how should you approach your first day of placement? What is expected of you? Well, read on to find out!

What (not) to wear!

This can be an agonizing choice, the source of much debate and discussion, and may well be the 'hot topic' on your PGCE course on the days leading up to placement. You may spend hours debating what to wear - what will make the right impression? What is appropriate? What will everyone else be wearing?

The answers to these questions partly depend on the age range and subject you are teaching but:-

Keep it professional, smart and sensible.

It goes without saying that you should never turn up for your first placement day looking like you are heading to the beach or about to spend a day in front of the TV!

Schools vary considerably when it comes to dress code - some will be strict "suit and tie" places, whereas others may be more relaxed. It is always better to be overdressed than too casual, so on your first day it'd be sensible to wear something like this:-

Males: - A pair of smart trousers, smart long sleeved shirt (tucked in!), jacket or blazer and a sensible tie.

Females: - Smart trousers or decent length skirt (plain) and a colourful blouse, shirt or jumper. (Courtesy of lots of female teachers on Twitter!)

Comfortable, smart shoes are a must (guys, put down those stilettos!) as you will be on your feet most of the day. Classrooms can also vary in temperature a lot (just add 30 hot and sweaty children to see what I mean!) so having layers is essential.

Schools will almost always request that any tattoos you may have are covered up and that you don't have excessive piercings (normally only ear piercings are 'allowed').

Guys - there is often a debate around ties - and you may well find that you don't have to wear one in your placement school (especially in primaries) - but wear one for your first day and you can always take it off if need be! Most schools will also request that you are clean shaven.

Girls - I'm reliably informed that you should avoid anything remotely low cut and always bend over in front of the mirror before you leave for school to make sure you can't see anything you shouldn't be able to! You should also bear in mind the school rule for ear piercings in pupils and try to stick to them - which normally means no dangly earrings. Needless to say there is no need for excessive makeup either!

After your first day you should be able to pick up on what is the 'norm' in your placement school. Remember you are representing the school whilst you are on placement so you have to adhere to what is expected from the school. You may notice your school is really informal - but even if other members of staff are wearing jeans and trainers it's best to avoid them yourself as a student teacher - especially when you have university tutors in etc.

Lots of advice came in from Twitterers about what to wear - so I'll leave the rest to them...

#pgcetips on.... What to wear!

Do not turn up to your placement wearing a crop top and hotpants. Even if you are studying to be a PE teacher. @Lisibo

Fashion advice for men. A silly tie dies not automatically make you 'down with the kids'. @chris_1974

...but a skinny tie and a stylish blazer does make you look very chic. @mark_howell101

Comfortable shoes will save your life! It's not a fashion show! Be modest in your attire. @purer_ethics

(fe)Male teachers also check your flies! #fortunatelynotpersonalexperience @chris_1974

Remember my pgce tutor (middle aged man) warning of dangers of wrong bra. He saw problems in cold weather! @vickitoria35

Female students - every new outfit you wear bend over and look in the mirror. If you can see expanses of bra try another outfit. @morphosaurus

Getting There

You should have found out from the school when you phoned them what time you should arrive, however if for any reason you haven't a good rule to follow is to arrive at least 30-40 minutes before the children are due to arrive.

You should obviously leave plenty of time for your journey on the first day - it is better to be early than to be late because you are stuck in traffic that everyone else at the school knows is always a problem! Schools generally won't mind you arriving early, but don't be offended if on the first day you are asked to wait in the staffroom - as your mentor/class teacher/head may not be in school yet or may be preparing for the lessons ahead.

Meeting Staff

Your first morning in the school will probably be full of lots of introductions to lots of different members of staff. This can be overwhelming - try to remember as much as you can (especially the key people like the head teacher, deputy head and receptionists!) but staff generally won't be offended if you have forgotten their name on the first day!

You should be introduced very quickly to your class teacher and/or mentor or student support teacher - these are going to be the most important people to you in the school and the people who will spend most time with you.

Always aim to introduce yourself to anyone new you meet – some staff may not be aware that the school has some student teachers on placement or may just generally be wondering who you are! Don't hide away from other staff members at breaks and lunch etc.

Most staff members will be really supportive and many will want to help you as much as they can - however don't be offended if a member of staff doesn't take any interest in you. At some point over your first few days it may be worth trying to work out or asking if the school has any NQTs and who at the school did their training at your training provider - these people are likely to be the most understanding and be willing to help, and will have recent memories of the course or teacher training too!

Meeting your class

[This is more geared at primary trainees but will be relevant to secondary too!]

Very soon after you arrive on your first day, you will probably find you meet the class that you will be spending your time in and eventually be teaching. This can be quite a daunting prospect - but the best piece of advice is to try to be relaxed.

Your class teacher may have already talked to your class about your imminent arrival, but this may not always be the case - your class teacher will have used their judgement to do what is best for their class.

If the school has given you a 'visitor' badge to wear - then try to make sure this is hidden from view when you are in the classroom with the children - you don't want them to see you as a 'visitor' - you want them to see you as a member of staff. Some schools will be stricter with this than others - but if you can manage to, try to get away from having to wear a visitor's badge (your class teacher/mentor may help sort this out for you)
.

Find out from your class teacher if they have to go and collect the children from the play-ground/elsewhere at the start of the school day - if so, ask if you can come out with them to collect the children.

When the children enter the classroom, you will probably be the first thing they notice - you are, after all, a new adult in their classroom! You will probably be faced with a barrage of questions from the children, normally along the lines of 'who are you?!?' - answer this as you feel comfortable - simply saying 'I'm Mr/Miss/Mrs X' may be sufficient - it is always a good idea to then ask the child's name and say how nice it is to meet them! You may also be asked 'Why are you here?!?' - again answer as you feel comfortable but you could say something along the lines of 'I'm going to be spending a lot of time with [class name] and I'm really looking forward to teaching you' (or similar!). Try to make sure you introduce yourself in the same way as the rest of the teaching staff at the school - which will normally be Mr/Mrs/Miss X.

Try not to stay glued to a seat at the back of the room! The children will probably have some form of early morning work to do whilst everyone arrives and the register is taken - try to mill around the classroom, looking at what the children are doing, helping if asked, and talking to the children.

The class teacher should hopefully also introduce you to the class as a whole after they have settled everything down - again you may be asked to introduce yourself - and it's often a good idea to add 'I'm really excited to be spending time with you all and am really looking forward to teaching you' - introducing yourself on your first day will probably be one of the scariest things you do on placement!

#pgcetips on.... Meeting your class

From The Tweeters

Remember that they are just as nervous as you on the first day! @Mrlockyer

There are so many people you need to be friends & nice to straight away but not the kids - you just need 2 b fair & honest 2 them @smckane

Front of class nerves evaporate if you focus your attention in your body rather than your mind - stops you from stressing out. @Cherylren

Learn pupil names - 1st lesson make a 'seating plan' and teach with it in your hand so that you can quickly refer to a pupil @qbhistory

What to do on your first day

Your training provider should give you guidance of what to do on your first day but the key piece of advice is:-

Get involved!

On your first day, don't just sit at the back of the classroom watching all day! Try to get stuck in - helping children, talking to them, and perhaps even working with a group during an activity. You will get to know the class much more quickly by doing this!

At some point during your first day, try to make sure you are given a tour of the school. If a member of staff shows you around, you may also want to see if you can ask for some volunteers from your class at break time to give you a tour as well - it's always interesting to get a child's perspective on the school and it can be a great opportunity to talk to and to get to know a group of children!

You should also make sure you have some time to discuss things with your class teacher/mentor on your first day - they will often be keen to discuss things with you too and you will probably have a list of things you need to find out or get sorted from your training provider. However understand that you may not get the chance to talk at length until after school. Make sure you have given your class teacher/mentor your contact details and try to get some contact details for them (e-mail will be a major help if they are willing!). Make sure you also have contact details for the school and save these to your phone.

Remembering Names...

However, one of your main jobs on the first day should be to try to remember the names of the children in your class. Knowing the names of the children in your class(es) will really help you build up a relationship with the class and will also give them a much better opinion of you - after all the last thing a child wants is for a teacher not to remember their name! Memorising names is a skill you will quickly develop as a teacher and you will develop a method that works best for you, but here are a few things to try:-

• Try to find out some information about each child - hopefully they will tell you something/a random fact that will help you remember them - for instance 'Rebecca who likes mountain biking' OR

• Try associating the child's name with something; sometimes doing this with a theme helps - for instance, if you chose an animal theme you could have 'crocodile Colin' – even better, try to get the chance to play a name game where you ask the children to introduce themselves and an animal (or something else) that begins with the letter of their first name.

• Simply repeating names and 'testing' yourself will also help - and the children will enjoy 'testing' you! Perhaps focus on remembering the names of a table at a time and making sure you know all the names before you allow yourself to move on. You could also challenge yourself to identify the children as the register is called etc...

You should also not be afraid of 'cheating' a little. If you can get a seating plan or create one yourself this will be a massive help (but be careful not to rely on it) - you can also be creative with how you find out names - a quick look at the front of a child's book, their pencil case, reading folder, top of their worksheet or anywhere else where their name will be written will often go unnoticed and the child will be surprised when you address them by name!

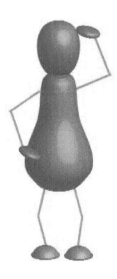

#pgcetips on.... *Your First Day*

What your mum told you still holds true today - pack your bag the night before you go to school enjoy those extra 5 min in bed! @Smckane

You planned what you'd wear to interview carefully do the same for your first week - set the tone for what the kids think of you! @Smckane

Don't forget the #pgtips on your first day!   @Missgembles

First day on placement: if you do nothing else learn all the pupils names - makes things so much easier to manage.   @oliverquinlan

I always bring goodies with me on my first visit to a school it makes entering the staffroom that little bit easier. @relativism

1st day - don't hide in department / staff room. Be prepared to be flexible. Know what you want to teach / observe   @mrgpg

1st day in schl. Ask where toilets are. Find out if you pay for coffee & how much. Ask about reprographics / resources. @chris_1974

Your handy guide to Support Staff

Receptionists, Caretakers, Technicians, Mid-Day Supervisors, Librarians, Bursars, and Teaching Assistants are just a few people who all fall under the blanket title of 'support staff' and put quite simply:-

Support staff are amazing!

Without the work of these people, a school could not function, and support staff are an integral part of the school.

One of the biggest tips for your placements is to get to know and respect your support staff. Spend a bit of time building up a relationship with your support staff and your placement is likely to be much easier! Here's a quick rundown of some of the support staff you will generally find in school and why you should get to know them!

Receptionists/Secretaries - Are often the eyes and ears of the school. They will invariably know what's going on, where stuff is, who is where and who is doing (or meant to be doing!) what. They are always good starting points and will be able to direct you to someone who can help. Receptionists will often know a lot of useful information about parents and children too! Most receptionists/secretaries will be all too happy to help - but bear in mind they are invariably very busy too! It is also worthwhile getting on your secretary's good side so that they are able to help when you jam the photocopier for the umpteenth time, manage to block the shredder or put jam in the laminator! Put simply - ignore receptionists/secretaries at your peril.

Caretakers and Cleaners - Will be working tirelessly before you arrive at school and after school has finished! It is thanks to your cleaners and caretakers that the school is 'restored' each evening! Get to know the cleaner who cleans your classroom and the caretaker! Don't take them for granted - always make sure you clean up after yourself and that your classes always leave the room tidy! Most importantly - if you have had a messy activity, or your classroom is in a particularly bad way - talk to your cleaner nicely, apologise profusely and offer to help! It's particularly important you tell them of any hidden 'spills' - the last thing you want is the smell of sour milk because you've forgotten to tell your cleaner someone spilt milk! Make sure you know what time your caretaker closes the school at night and always make sure you are out by then! Caretakers and cleaners are often also an excellent source of friendly conversation!

Mid-Day Supervisors - Are the people who allow the teaching staff to take a break at lunchtime! Always respect your mid-day supervisors and listen to any concerns they may have about your placement class. When you begin to take over more responsibility for your class, make sure you always follow up any issues arising from lunchtime with your class and try to check once in a while that everything is ok!

Technicians - Come in many 'varieties' but ICT and Science technicians are probably the most common. If you are teaching in one of these areas in a secondary school your relationship with your technician will be key - but don't treat them as general dogsbodies! If you are in a primary school you will probably find that you have an ICT technician visit frequently and they are the people who will try to help you resolve any ICT issues you have - so make sure you introduce yourself to them!

Bursars - Are an increasingly common sight in schools and are the people who look after the financial side of the school. Much of what has already been said about receptionists also applies to bursars. Bursars are also handy to know as they can sort out any problems to do with money - if you are organising a trip they are also often your first port of call - but as a student teacher it's advisable to check anything to do with school finances with your mentor first before approaching the bursar.

Teaching assistants - Are the support staff who you will probably work with most frequently, and if you build up a good relationship with them and respect them, they can be a major help to you. As teaching assistants are so important we'll cover working with teaching assistants later on.

Regardless of which members of support staff you come across, always make sure you treat them with the respect and gratitude they deserve and it will pay dividends!

#pgcetips on.... Support Staff

Get to know the support staff they often have valuable inside knowledge @nellmog

Get to know your classroom cleaner VERY WELL - and apologise if you make a lot of mess!   @Billgibbon

listen to the support staff and make them feel included - they will know the school procedures   @trudianns

TAs/LSAs etc are people too. They are too often treated as lower humans by teachers- don't let yourself fall into this trap.   @TeaKayB

Keep the support staff sweet. Especially lab technicians. They are also great sources of advice. Talk to them. @Dannynic

If you plan to do cool stuff with ed tech a conversation with your school's network manager or technician will be time well spent @mberry

be nice to TAs and keep them informed of stuff about kids & day to day stuff in school. (from my sis a TA who won't do twitter!)   @chris_1974

Your Working Hours.

When you are on placement it goes without saying that you should treat your placement as a full time job. You should expect to be in school before the children arrive and leave after the children finish.

Most teachers tend to arrive at least half an hour before the children enter school - this gives you time to sort things out for your lessons that day, prepare the classroom and make sure you are all organised. Some people prefer to come into school much earlier than this, and ultimately you need to do what feels best. It is always good to try to be at school around the time your class teacher or mentor arrives. Often schools hold briefings (either whole school or year teams) before school - make sure you find out the days of these and that you are in school for these.

As a minimum, just like qualified teachers, you should be entitled to 10% of a full time teacher's timetable off timetable (so around 2.5 hours each full week) but your training provider will set out guidelines as to how much 'non contact' time you should get and it will often be considerably more than this, especially in your earlier days of placement. Make sure you get this time and that you use it well - it is initially designed for planning, preparation and assessment (PPA), but as a trainee you may also want to use it to complete your evaluations and paperwork!

After school, many teachers choose to stay for considerable amounts of time to mark, plan and run after school clubs. You should expect to stay behind at least half an hour after the children have left, but be prepared to need to stay much longer. Some trainees prefer to do planning at school and others prefer to do it at home but you should aim to leave school with most things prepared and ready for the next day. Most schools hold a staff meeting after school, often once a week - find out when this is and try to go along to it (but check this is ok first) - you will often find out useful information that will affect you on placement and it is also a good experience to have. Later on in your placements it is also worthwhile trying to get involved in, or set up your own, after-school club - it is great experience to have and looks great on job applications!

#pgcetips on.... Time Management

Plan your time efficiently to make sure you have a good work/life balance
No one likes or respects a burned-out martyr! @lauradoggett

You WILL be working at night and on weekends. Get used to it! :o)
@4goggas

RT @4goggas: You WILL be working at night and on weekends. Get used
to it! :o) <-- But it'll be worth it   @ianaddison

Know the value of prioritising and be strong enough to say no. @cjs76

get your classroom practice sorted before you launch into running lots of
xtra curricular clubs @clairelowe2

Adapt / use resources already created - there is often no need to re-invent
the wheel - save your energy for teaching!   @ZoeRoss19

remember that time management is essential - it's a very busy year!
@AndyRoss75

The Staffroom

Staffrooms come in all shapes and sizes - from tiny rooms with 4 chairs in a small primary to large, cavernous spaces in large secondary schools!

Regardless of the shape of your staffroom, as a student you should always make sure you try to show your face - the last thing you want is to be seen as some mysterious being who is never seen beyond the classroom. Try to get to the staffroom at lunch, and at break if you are free too. As well as being a good opportunity to meet and talk to other staff, a trip to the staffroom will provide a much needed break from the classroom.

Staffrooms can be quite a daunting place for the 'uninitiated' so here are some handy tips!

Don't just use any mug - make sure you find out on your first day what the arrangements with regards to mugs are! You'll probably find that staff have their own mug - so make sure you do too, but there may also be some visitors mugs for you to use on your first day (look for the old, dingy mugs!). The last thing you want is the wrath of a teacher who finds out that someone had used their mug!

Find out about the arrangements for tea, coffee and milk! What appears to be a relatively simple task of sorting out supplies for the staff room can often take up hours at staff meetings, and in some schools someone walking in and using the sacred supplies without asking is nearly enough to spark World War 3! Find out if you have to opt in and pay to use the communal 'supplies', if all staff are expected to contribute or if you have to supply your own. Above all always offer to contribute.

Make sure you are not sitting in someone else's 'seat' - this is especially so in large secondary schools - you will often find out that departments sit in a certain area of the staffroom and that sometimes a teacher will always sit in the same seat - make sure you are not upsetting the status quo!

Use one seat - don't make a habit of spreading your stuff out over more than one seat. Seats are often in short supply.

Never eat the last piece of chocolate cake. Remember all that healthy eating stuff you try to encourage in the children? Well it doesn't apply in the staffroom! You will often find there will be biscuits, cakes, chocolate and other sweet things in the staffroom (so basically all the things the school probably bans from the children's packed lunches!) Often this will be because it's someone birthday but some schools also have a day where staff take it in turns to supply 'goodies' for the staffroom. By all means, enjoy the treats, and it's always a good thing to buy some treats once in a while for the staffroom - but never take the last piece – or else you may find yourself the centre of a major investigation!

Clean up after yourself. It goes without saying that you should always make sure you clear away your rubbish but always make sure you do your washing up or load your cup into the dishwasher.

Be aware of who's in the staffroom. Teachers often talk about their class and problems they are having with them in the staffroom - but before you say anything make sure it's appropriate and you know who is around - the last thing you want is to complain about a pupil and find out their parent is a member of staff and is standing right behind you!

Be prepared for any conversation! No topic is off limits in a staffroom. Men who are in a primary staffroom which often have a predominately female staff should be most aware of this. Be prepared to shield your ears (or join in if you want!) for conversations which may include waxing, periods, giving birth, sex and much more!

Watch how long other people stay in the staffroom. You'll rarely find a teacher who stays in the staffroom all lunchtime - after all you will probably have some preparation to do for the afternoon's lessons. Keep an eye on how long other members of teaching staff generally stay in the staffroom and try to follow suit!

#pgcetips on.... The Staffroom!

Don't be cheesed off if staff don't bother getting to know you - make an effort to go to people. Others might not.
@mfl_noemie

#pgcetips Dont hide away in the staffroom. Get fully involved in the life of your school. Get to know students beyond ur lessons (& SMILE)
@JamiePortman

Find out school position on areas / mugs etc.
@chris_1974

Be careful where you sit in the staffroom. Stay away fromthe energy sappers. You'll spot them quickly!
@Smichael920

In the staffroom mix as much as poss. Talk to other subject areas all students TA's especially.   @chris_1974

Remember NEVER to be like the 'blockers' who breathe negativity each day in the staffroom; your energy will inspire others!
@DeputyMitchell

Observing Teaching

One of the main things you will find yourself doing during your placements is observing other teachers teaching. This is a fantastic opportunity and one not to be missed, as at no other time in your career will you get so much time to observe and learn from others. Throughout your PGCE you are likely to see a wide variety of teachers, teaching strategies and approaches, and if used effectively these will significantly aid your development as a teacher. Most of the time you will probably find you will gain equally as much being an active part and assisting in the lesson as you will being a 'passive' observer - so don't feel that you have to sit and just watch when you are observing!

You probably be keen to observe when you start your placement, but when you are taking on an increasing teaching timetable on placement it is easy to feel that it is not beneficial to be spending your time observing - after all, you'd probably rather be teaching yourself! But you should still take the opportunity to observe others as this can help you in areas which you have identified as needing development and you should focus your observations in these development areas.

It is also hugely beneficial to experience and observe as many teachers' practice as you can - it goes without saying that every teacher teaches differently and you will benefit from exposure to a wide range of styles. It is equally helpful and interesting to observe other year groups and, if you can, key stages, and this can really help you see the development of children.

But how exactly do you observe a lesson? Your training provider should give you some guidance but here are a few tips:-
•Decide if you have a focus for your observation - are you particularly looking at how the teacher manages transitions for example? If you have a focus, try to stick to the focus.
•Talk to the teacher you are observing beforehand - make sure they are happy with you being in the lesson and if they want you to base yourself in a particular place etc.
•Unless the teacher you are observing asks you to, don't just sit in the back of the classroom, move around the room and interact with the children.
•If you do sit down, try to avoid sitting in the teacher's direct eye line.
•Writing copious notes can be very off-putting for the teacher - so try to avoid doing this if at all possible; instead, try to remember key things and make notes as soon as you can after the lesson.
•Your reflections afterwards are important. If you have set a focus for the observation you should try to reflect on this. If you were just generally observing, you may want to think about things like how the teacher approached the lesson, what teaching styles they used and how they responded to specific 'incidents'.
•After the lesson you may find it helpful to discuss the lesson with the teacher - but whatever you do, DO NOT tell the teacher they did something wrong or tell them they could have done it better by doing Y. You should also avoid passing judgement on the lesson in any way - do not, for example, say, 'I thought that was a good lesson'.

Always remember you are not an OFSTED inspector and you are observing to learn from the teacher, not to 'assess' the teacher.

#pgcetips on.... Observing Teaching

Make time to go and observe other teachers in the school and don't be scared to ask about things.   @squiggle7

If you have difficulties with a particular class observe them with another teacher in a different setting.   @MarkAMacInnes

observe as many lessons as possible. Across different subjects - so many ideas to be adapted!   @purer_ethics

Don't just watch the good teachers watch someone who's training or got a difficult class. You also need to learn what NOT to do @mandared

Listen observe and ask questions @tonycassidy

Don't be too quick to judge- the difference between theory and practice is often a result of circumstance   @tonycassidy

Try to observe other teachers' classes and make notes on specific things: communication; use of group work etc   @Caro_lann

Even more #pgcetips on.... Observing Teaching!

Would advise seeing outstanding teachers across the school. Don't copy them but you will learn lots about obs success   @mark_howell101

When observing ask:"why is it going well"" (or badly!?). What are the students doing? What is the teacher doing? (in that order)" @chris_1974

Don't be afraid to get in & mingle with pupils during obs; kids expect adults in classroom to do this!   @marketspi

When obs note how teacher uses time and diff activities in diff segments of lesson e.g. individual pair group writing drama @rantingteacher

Volunteer to take out small groups of pupils as focus group. It helps establish confidence as a teacher and rapport with pupils.   @Marketspi

Observe outstanding teachers but try to observe some that are seen to be not so good. You will learn a lot from both.   @Oliverquinlan

It is one of THE most helpful things I've ever done to sit in and observe other teachers' classes just for ideas and tips.   @morphosaurus

Classroom Management

By Ryan Delaney

Picture this: you have spent the best part of the past year selecting, applying and being interviewed for a limited place on an over subscribed teacher training programme. If like me you're on the mad side and the day comes when you find out you have been successful and offered a place on a PGCE course you run around the house with pure joy knowing that you're definitely going to enjoy the tough year ahead. You'll notice I have said tough. How can it be any tougher than the honours year of your undergraduate course? Well to be frank: have you ever had to manage 30 young disinterested students before, as well as deliver a top notch inspirational lesson, face a constant barrage of assessment, criticism and anything else nasty about a teaching practice? No, didn't think so. Here is where I can help with some tips about classroom management. You will (and you should) be well read up on education theory, be up to date with the latest eduction initiatives, know the real reasons why that year 10 student just doesn't want to do any work in your class and persists on making your life pure hell or why that 5 year old boy just cries the minute he steps into your room and persists on screaming for his "mummy" and know the "proper" way of dealing with that, backed up by theory. However, let me give you some tried and tested tips.

Before I begin I will make one personal belief of mine crystal clear: you are in a classroom with children who do not know you from Adam, you have been assigned to a teacher who can and will make your life very difficult if they want (and you allow it) but what you must remember is that you are there to be "teacher" not "classroom assistant". If, when you have class responsibility something kicks off and it's you and a classroom assistant in the room it becomes your responsibility to get the class back in order, so learn how to do that as quickly as you can. How do you do it? Simple: watch, observe and ask questions of your class teacher from day one. This has many benefits: it shows you are interested, shows you are willing to learn their way (even if you know it's wrong- smile and nod) and makes that teacher feel more valued than this know it all student they have had thrown on them. After you have begun to build this trust the class teacher will become more confident in allowing you to implement your own methods. It is important you do this for a variety of reasons: their way may be dated and could lose you credentials on your tutor visit, their method may simply be too dramatic a performance like for a shy student like yourself and this time next year it's going to be you and your own class with no teacher to observe and take over. As a rule of thumb always give the teacher the direct opportunity to slate your method and tell you why it just didn't work (make sure there are no students in the room when this happens!)

First thing is first: before you have little people or big people in your classroom you need to decide how you want to appear to them. For a second think back to your own school days. Remember any little, timid trainee sitting at the back with their note book? Not really interacting much? Well please do not be this trainee. From day one make sure you are dressed to kill, that you are visible to them (preferably not sitting as they enter) If it's you taking the class be standing at the door. Say "good morning" (followed by a name if you know it) but try not to get into any long conversation. If it's the class teacher taking the lesson, and you are observing stand in the middle of room ready to give instructions as the teacher does something else. By saying something as simple "Quickly boys. Jackets off, pencil case out!" immediately establishes you as an authority figure. The point here is that you are welcoming the students into your space, and keeping an eye on what's happening in the classroom and in the corridor. And please, don't have your arms folded. If you are feeling nervous put them in your pockets.

As the wonderful Lady Marie Stubbs once said "You should sit down and decide what makes a good education for the children. Every child should be intrinsically valued". If you do decide to take Stubbs up on her advice (I highly recommend that you do) give a lot of your thinking time to how children can feel valued within your classroom management. Do you want children to feel that they belong in your room or that they are merely a guest? - two important things to consider. In my own experience I have changed opinions many times (and you will too, depending on the class and their behaviour)

It is commonly known that primary teachers have wonderful organisational skills who keep bright and tidy classrooms. If this is the case perhaps the secondary teachers amongst us can learn a thing or two about organising and managing your very first classroom. Go into a primary classroom and you should see a tidy, well organised room with everything smeared in a label (something similar to comic sans font, of course). Go into a secondary classroom and you will most likely see a bit of a mess, walls poorly decorated and very little sign of a teacher owning the room. I think we need to learn something from your primary colleagues on this one. Think about the direct messages we are sending to students if they are learning in an environment where there are high expectations of the way it looks and feels. Ask to take on something to do with a display on teaching practice. Design a wonderfully stimulating context display. As teachers we can sometimes want displays to be purely a showcase of students "best" work. I think it's better to utilise the limited wall space as a showcase of learning notes that will aid the students further in their learning.

As you start your forward planning for your responsibility think about the resources you are going to need. What textbooks? How many jotters? Is there a whole school policy on the type of jotter used for a particular subject? After you have answers to these questions ensure you are proactive and have them in your classroom ready to start. The students will see it as a sign of weakness if the first few lessons have you leaving the room to get things. Ask any experienced practitioner how to lay out the desks and they will be very quick to tell you it depends on the class/classes using the room and that you will change your mind a dozen times within the one school session. To see the desks in rows in a Primary school will be an unusual sight, however there are primary teachers out there who will use this method. "Rows" are still a very common feature of a secondary classroom. Whatever method you use ensure you can justify it in terms of teaching and learning. The table overleaf can be used to look at the advantages and disadvantages of each model.

Model	Why is this good?	Any Downsides?
Mixed ability/Social Groupings	Creates movement as children have to move around for specific teaching inputs. More able students assist less able.	Can cause disruption Distribution of resources for different abilities.
Rows	Children are facing forwards, which can cause less disruption and time during teacher led activities to ensure "all eyes are forward"	Children do need to learn to work independently, does this allow this? Teacher can't easily walk around the classroom Co-operative learning can not be easily factored into lessons. Teacher becomes the main resour Resources are difficult to share if they are already limited.
Horseshoe.	No where for the child to hide. This gives the teacher a full glance of everyone. Useful for lessons which involve debate	Need a large space.

Okay, so in an ideal situation would be you going into a class, giving them a democratic voice in making up class rules and spending a good couple of months enforcing rule after rule and letting very little slip. The sad reality is you are going into a classroom where rules have (or should have been) well established and everything running like clockwork for the students and their class teacher. Then the teacher and students need to adjust to a student and vice versa. You have just around four school weeks to have a positive impact on the students you teach, and hopefully leave having passed the placement. Well, my advice is simply familiarise yourself from the minute you step into the school/class what the general expectations of behaviour are. Ensure you enforce them straight away. I have had the pleasure of speaking to many teachers about what they like to see from a student. And time after time they say they want a student who looks and acts like a teacher, not the students pal. If you notice that the teacher can have a joke with their class and then enforce rules a second later but you can't, do not worry. You need to remember that teacher has had that first few months that I discussed above to establish their expectations, sadly placement doesn't give you that luxury. Make sure you have an idea of how you would get the class silent if you had to. I use a rhythmic clap that children repeat, then I would reward points to the group who fell silent the quickest (no one is too old for points and a prize)

After all the rule making ensure you have made sure that children know how the classroom runs; where are things kept? Where does finished work go? Who hands books out? All these routines need to established as quickly as possible. If you manage this then you will most definitely be on your way to a very successful start in the next chapter of your professional life. You will make mistakes. You will cry. You will get fed up and want to throw the towel in but as my very first school experience tutor told me "have a good cry in the toilet, brush your self down and then get on with it, with a smile if you can manage one"

Teaching Your First Lesson
By Mark Howell

Without doubt teaching your first lesson is one of the biggest landmarks in your PGCE year and indeed one of the biggest in your career. You will have built up to it for some time and have probably spent more time planning it than you will ever spend planning another lesson. It is very likely that you will know the class you are teaching as you should have had the chance to observe them with their regular class teacher. You should therefore know a few of the characters and they should know you, you should have a vague understanding of the class dynamic and be aware of the lesson formats they are used to. It seems to me to be a certainty that the regular class teacher would be there, meaning that behaviour standards are likely to be similar to what you saw on your observation (after all, any problems at this stage your mentor or class teacher observing you will be dealing with them). You may even have taught a starter or plenary or even team-taught a lesson with that class. Therefore, with expectations already known to students, familiarity with you and decent behaviour standards you should be in a position to just get teaching, right from the start.

I decided to look back at my early feedback reports from my PGCE year in order to write this and reflect on some of the successes and failures of my early lessons. This should provide some very rough dos and don'ts for your first lesson.

Students will come to the lesson and expect things to be as normal. I recommend you try not to disrupt this normal pattern as they will already be a little off guard by having a new teacher. To start changing routine as well may not be the most productive use of your and their time. So if they normally line up outside, let them do this, and if they come in as and when, let them do this. I would also stick to any seating plan that already exists. You will most likely have a copy of this and be beginning to learn who sits where. Having a new teacher will prompt a few of them to ask to move. Make sure you don't budge on this and keep them all sat exactly where they normally do. The same may not be said for the register. I always found with new classes that formally taking a register at the start brings a nice early focus to the lesson and gets them quietly listening to you. Once the register is complete you can immediately start the lesson as they are already focussed on you. It of course has the added benefit of helping to learn a few more names. Some teachers prefer to do a covert register part way through the lesson, so they may not be expecting it at the start. Once you think most of them are in and sat down calmly ask for them to be quiet and remain quiet whilst you go through the register.

Although, as stated above, you should be in a position to hit the ground running straight away, I would always start with a quick 5 minute brief on who you are and what you expect. This is something I have done since my first ever lesson and continue to do now. Tell them who you are and leave your name written on the board on display as they will forget. It is then important to set out a brief expectation of them even if your mentor has already done so. At this stage you will most likely not know the specifics of what you will and will not allow in class so you need to tell them that you expect them to have the same levels of behaviour and same work ethics as they have with their normal class teacher. Now, at this stage it is unlikely that you will be able to enforce such standards but it is important to let them know that you intend for them to work and to behave. You and your mentor will work over the coming weeks and months on how to establish those standards for yourself. Following this I always took 2 minutes out to explain a bit about my background. In school I frequently used to question why I should listen to my teachers and what authority they had on the topics being learned about. I usually show students a few slides of me on Mont Blanc and tell them about my degree and how it has enabled me to travel a bit and do research. I find this often gets them excited about geography, if only for a few minutes but more importantly lets them know that I know what I am talking about and you quickly develop a air of authority at least in terms of subject knowledge if not class management.

At this point you will probably kick off what will be a very well prepared starter. Of course this should be a task which can easily be explained and lasts only a few minutes. Try to make this task either recap on previous learning or lead into what will be done today. In early lessons I had success with paired activities getting students to do either card sorts or taboo cards or something similar which allows them to do some discussion. These activities also allow you to circulate and encourage any pairs or groups who may be off task. In early lessons I would avoid whole class starters whilst you get to know names and whilst you improve your management skills. Once you have completed the starter be sure to reflect briefly on it, how does it relate to previous learning or how does it relate to what we will do today.

You are then ready to move onto the main part of your lesson. Even the most unruly classes will normally give new teachers a chance to talk in the early lessons, especially with their usual class teacher in the room. My second PGCE placement school was notoriously challenging and I was surprised how each new class I taught gave me the opportunity, at least in my first lesson, to address them without any challenging behaviour. Try to be firm and do address any students who fall out of line but at the same time I found that students will respond well to you being relaxed and enthusiastic. Many teachers will tell you not to smile until Christmas and I am sure this is very successful for some people. I personally feel that students listen to me because they are interested in what I have to say and not because they are scared of the consequences of not listening to me. This has only come about by having a class atmosphere which encourages engagement and enjoyment of the subject.

I found that early on powerpoints [or IWB files] were a great safety blanket for introducing the lesson. You can make them visually exciting and enable you to almost script what you want to say to students. Be careful not to include too much text on the powerpoint and do not make them last too long. One thing which I found is easy to do early on is to continue talking even if some students are not listening. This is a problem which will grow unless nipped in the bud so right from the start do not say anything unless you have silence. You will develop your own methods of dealing with those not listening but try a few things early on (the stare will normally suffice).

Then you will of course have planned a task for them to do; whether it be a worksheet, group task or textbook work, make sure you model the task effectively. Clearly explain what you want them to do and leave it written up or up on powerpoint throughout the task. At the end be sure to ask if anybody is not sure what they need to be doing. If 1 student is confused it is likely that more are. They should then get on with what you have asked them to do and will likely be at their usual levels of focus. If that is not the case you may have to stop them working and remind them of your expectations before allowing them to continue. Make sure you have an extension planned as some students will finish and it is a painful feeling in your early lessons to have all the bright students sat there with nothing to do for 10 minutes, it is an even worse feeling to have a class sat there with nothing to do for 10 minutes. Sometimes tasks just don't take as long as you plan so make sure you have something as a backup.

Be sure to allow time to review the task and answers to any questions set. As you will have circulated during the task you will have seen some good work and it is always good to share this by getting some students to share their answers. You should have allowed time for a plenary at the end which should review the leaning of the day. Make sure you finish with 2 or 3 minutes to spare in order to allow students to pack away, tidy the room and stand quietly waiting for the bell. Many new teachers struggle with rushed ends to their lessons early on so do allow enough time for all the tidying to take place and you can then formally dismiss students.

#pgcetips on.... Teaching (generally)

Routines! Starts and ends of lessons are crucial. Stick to your routine for orderly beginnings and endings
@simonhowells

Dont feel daunted about C management. Invest in the students and they will invest in you. Find out about their interests &SMILE!
@JamiePortman

eEidence evidence evidence. Observe record classify and reference as you go.
@Billgibbon

Practise projecting your voice at home. You may feel silly but it will be worth it.
@Mathsatschool

Be prepared to stay at school late: your mentor and others will have more time to help
@afawnie

Be observant organised & calm. Learn from both the good & bad you see & collect ideas and resources like a magpie.   @Wizenedcrone

Your Class Teacher/Mentor
By Mark Howell

In all probability you will become very close to your mentor during your time in school.

Your first impression is important. My first mentor has since openly admitted to me that he thought I would be rubbish at teaching from the moment we met right up until the point I taught my first lesson. He said when I walked in the room with unkempt long hair, ripped jeans and a lip piercing he feared the worst. Thankfully I was always enthusiastic and so he kept faith in me long enough for me to demonstrate that I was probably going to be better than rubbish. On first meeting be confident and enthusiastic about the challenges ahead but avoid being arrogant, which obviously never goes down well with someone who has much much more experience than you. Try to learn about the school, the department and the catchment in that first meeting.

In the early stages, before you start teaching, try to spend as much time in class with them as possible. Firstly be helpful, help students out, help keep an eye on or even manage unruly students and ask questions after lessons as to why certain things were done in certain ways. All this will be helpful when you come to taking the class for yourself.

You will be likely to see your mentor teach a number of times before you start teaching yourself. They are likely to be an experienced teacher who is held in some regard in the school and it is very easy to just want to copy what they do. Whilst you should take notes on how they operate and try to pick up as many tips as possible, do not try to be just like them. You need to be yourself in a class and have your own style and so therefore avoid acting just like them.

My 2 mentors were very different, and as such I had to be quite a different teacher in my 2 placements. Possibly this was down to experience, possibly down to them trying to get me to fit into the ethos and requirements of operating in very different environments and possibly this was just down to their very different styles. My first mentor was very relaxed in class management but also a really interesting guy who the kids really liked. He emphasised getting along with the kids and teaching really interesting lessons (I remember him saying "if I am bored so are they, so make it interesting") but by OFSTED standards my lessons in first placement were well short of the mark. He did fill me with lots of confidence and that was a good thing in the early stages. My second mentor was by the book and had been training teachers for 20 years. Lessons plans, learning objectives, class management were all dot every I and cross every T. Whilst it took a little adjustment, I realised this was what I needed after my first one and the combination of the 2 made me better than had I been with just one. Barely a day goes by, though, where I do not remember some piece of advice or wisdom passed on by both of them. My point to take from this really is regardless of the extent to which you get along with your mentor and regardless of how much their style may differ from yours, you will learn a great deal just from operating around them. **You may not even realise their impact until you begin the NQT year fending for yourself**

Mentors - a few extra bits for Primary Students.

All of Mark's advice holds true for those doing a Primary PGCE, but here are a few extra points just for Primary PGCE students:-

•Your mentor is likely to be the class teacher of the class you are placed in and they will normally be teaching this class for the majority of the school week.

•You will probably see your mentor/class teacher teach a considerable number of lessons before you start to teach and you may then start to share lessons with them.

•'Your' placement class is really your class teacher's class - you should always bear this in mind and be respectful of this. If you want to make any major changes to the way things are done in the class, make sure you discuss them with your class teacher/mentor first, after all they will have to teach the class 'full time' again when you leave.

•On very rare occasions, you may find you experience difficulties with your mentor for one reason or another. Make sure that if you find yourself in this situation, you let your university or course tutor know as soon as possible. They will be able to give you good advice and support.

#pgcetips on.... Your Class Teacher/Mentor

Don't try to be a clone of your mentor! @chris_1974

If you don't feel you are getting the support you should from your mentor don't suffer in silence. @Cloudlilly

If you THINK you know the answer you don't! Don't act on something if you are not 100% sure. Check with your mentor. @ColinTGraham

Don't be afraid to ask for help and if it isn't forthcoming ask someone else @vikkiiom

Don't go on pment thinking you know it all listen to the teachers yr working with you may have ideas but it's still their class @amweston

Use your department head as a guide you don't have to do everything on your own no matter how busy they may appear. @4Goggas

Don't mistake well intentioned help with criticism. Be open to others suggestions you may not act on it but it shows they care   @Smichael920

Even more #pgcetips on.... Your Class Teacher

value input of your school-based mentor + fill your boots with as many school experiences - trips/parent meetings etc - as you can   @stevewn

Let your mentor know sooner rather than later if you are struggling! @shellbelle21

there is no such thing as a stupid question (for you or kids) the longer you leave it the harder it will be to ask.   @chris_1974

listen to others perspectives and take on board their advice but make your own judgements about what works well too   @squiggle7

Learn from your mentor but don't try and be your mentor. Find out what works for you.   @prettejohn

You can learn something from everyone. Even people who you don't see eye-to-eye with. Sometimes a bad model is more revelatory. @Lauradoggett

Listen to advice you're offered. Then weigh it up. Remember you might not know it all but you're not completely clueless @lisibo

Behaviour Management

Behaviour management is often an area of concern for trainee teachers and is probably one of the areas you will develop most in during the course.

Some basic tips are provided here by Jenny Harvey and Gerald Haigh, but nothing can really replace the experience gained from being in a school and observing teachers and how they deal with behaviour management. Books that provide specific advice on behaviour management for different age groups are also available - ask your training provider for recommendations.

Behaviour: taming the monkeys - By Jenny Harvey

You can (and should) read about many different behaviour management techniques but the real learning will come kinaesthetically, through practice.

Leave self consciousness in the car park: If you have inhibitions about implementing techniques such as clapping and singing try not to focus on the performance aspect. It is much easier to become a teacher in front of pupils than it is around other adults. Forget about who else is in the classroom with you and focus on the pupils.

Practise varying your tone before you step foot in a classroom: I often use my teacher voice at home with family, friends and occasionally in the supermarket! While this isn't advisable it is very useful to experience the impact your tone has on others.

Positivity breeds ethos: Positive measures in reinforcing desired behaviour are more effective than dealing with the aftermath of a classroom revolt. "You catch more bees with honey" will strike a chord here.

Remember your role: Try not to do everything at once and definitely do not make the mistake of being a friend to your pupils. Building a relationship based on solid guidelines and respect will serve you far better when you need to enforce school policies or set work that is unfavourable.

Know your environment: Know your school, classroom, pupils, class teacher and school policies well. If you have a sound knowledge of these everything else clicks together much easier.

Finally: It just happens! This may sound like a cliché but when you are in the classroom, over your pre-lesson nerves and doing what you have been born to do things come together. You have read, researched, practised and planned for this and being prepared is being the best you can be. Things will rarely go to plan, problems will happen and you need to be flexible, but this is when you truly learn and develop your teaching skills, so enjoy the ups and learn the downs.

Gerald Haigh's top behaviour tips.

Learn at least some of the names in advance, and be ready to use them at the first opportunity.

Be at your first session ahead of the children. If the rule is they wait at the door for you, make sure that in fact you're at the door ready for them. If they have no fixed places, direct them to seats. Don't get into arguments.

At the first encounter with a class don't go into chatty mood. Instead of that actually BE a teacher straight away, to fix children on the idea that a teacher is what you are. Give a task immediately. Make it simple and interesting. Make sure the children have everything they need to do it with – you don't want lots of questions and faffing about. As they work, smile and immediately give praise – "You're working well John, plenty of concentration there Ramandeep, well done."

Then the chattiness comes afterwards as you discuss the task. The aim of this is to establish that you are definitely the teacher, that you're there to teach, and that you know what you're doing. You therefore live up to their basic expectation, which is "You're the teacher, so teach us."

Mark the work quickly and talk about it, again giving praise and any merit marks that the school uses.

Remember all the time that praise works wonders. If you find a class over-excited and slow to settle, try not to shout, "Settle down now"…Instead, fix on the ones that are getting the point. "Yes, here's someone who's ready to get on, well done. And over there, another who's already ahead of everybody else……" Keep doing that and they'll all quickly subside. That's so much better than generally yelling for quiet, which is something to avoid.

Establish your own brand – the way you set out your online tasks, the use of your name, and perhaps a little avatar. Use phrases that they'll remember for ever. "

If you have a really difficult child, don't get into angry confrontations in front of the class. See him or her afterwards. When you do, again make clear you're the teacher. Set out the rules of your relationship, making clear that you'll listen to anything said to you politely and at an appropriate time, but that you're setting the framework for what goes on in class. Keep eye contact, be assertive but not aggressive.

If there's real trouble, refer it upwards quickly and frankly. Don't hide anything. If you did anything wrong – blurt out an inappropriate thing in anger for example – be frank about it. Leadership don't want anything to come out later.

#pgcetips on.... Behaviour Management

Don't take it personally: remember that bad behaviour is the solution for the kid not the problem. Try to figure out the root. @MrsThorne

Don't paint yourself into corners with classes never promise or threaten - stop digging when you are already in a hole! @didactylos

Be clear about the rewards and sanctions policy and use them both. @lisibo

Don't expect to do a lot of subject teaching unless you're a real expert at classroom management.   @ColinTGraham

Don't be too smug if you can control a class that experienced teachers have problems with!   @Vickiesheridan

Communicate frequently with parents particularly if child has or causes probs. Phone/ note in diary/ parentmail/ letter.   @purer_ethics

Consistency.   @shellbelle21

Even more #pgcetips on....
Behaviour Management

You will get excuses. A person can on;ly have two grandmothers and they can each die only once. My record is five!   @JohnColby

A class vote gets hands up. Once you have got them used to the idea once or twice then more direct questions can follow.   @JohnColby

If you need to do a seating plan ask the TA to help - they know the kids well enough to make it work!   @Mandared

n't leave school till you've dealt with any student issues that occurred during the day. Even if loads shows you mean business!
@Graemesmith1978

Treat pupils with respect and they are more likely to respect you back.
@MarkAMacInnes

Stickers, stickers and more stickers! A bell shaker also for the younger ones works wonders in rapidly silencing a classroom of noisy capers!
@Portesh

When behaviour management is going down the pan: Remember they're children and they just want to have fun.   @roseski_

Planning

Planning will probably take up lots of your time - but what exactly is it and how do you approach it?

What is Planning?
Put simply - planning is the process of deciding what will teach and how you will teach it. Planning can be long term (covering a term or year), medium term (covering a unit or half term), weekly or daily (in which you set out in detail your plans for a lesson). On your PGCE you will produce hundreds of daily plans and should also need to get experience producing medium term plans (but this won't come until later on in the year).

Why Plan?
Planning is essential for effective teaching - especially when you are training. Lessons will generally be most effective when you have given thought to the content, learning objectives and activities. You also need to be able to demonstrate you can plan effectively to gain QTS.

What do you plan?
During your teacher training you will be expected to produce individual lesson plans for every lesson you teach. Your training provider will expect to see these when they come to visit you in school and your class teacher/mentor will also expect daily plans. Especially towards the end of your training, make sure you keep on top of your planning and plan as you go along (rather than producing the plans after the lesson as some trainees do!).

What do you need to include?
Your training provider will tell you exactly what they expect to see in your plans, but in daily plans you should as a minimum include:-

The Learning Objective(s) - what do you want the children to learn from the lesson? These should normally follow on and build on the previous lesson or the children's prior skills and knowledge and will also normally be linked to the national curriculum or other non-statutory guidance (strategies etc). Try to keep the learning objective small and achievable - this is not the place to state long term goals. As an example a maths lesson may have a primary learning object of "Children will be able to partition three digit numbers"

The Success Criteria - What are you looking for from the children? [NB - it can be equally as effective to develop this with the children - see the assessment section] – this shouldn't just be the learning objective in child friendly language! Try to be specific; for the example above, it could be "I can partition 478 in Hundreds, Tens and Units"

Assessment - How are you going to assess the lesson? See the assessment section for more guidance.

Resources - What resources do you need for the lesson? Write them down so you can make sure you have everything you need.

Session Outline - What is going to happen in the session? You should set out the activities that will help the children achieve the success criteria you have set out. In a 'typical' lesson this will normally include some 'shared learning' (i.e. teacher led learning) and either group work and/or independent learning - but plan what will work best for your lesson. Avoid 'scripting' the lesson in your session outline - this can remove the spontaneity of a lesson and children will never say what you have 'planned' for them to say!

Additional Adults - What role are any additional adults (Teaching Assistants, Parents etc) going to have in your lesson?

How do you plan?

Planning is personal - it is not something that can be done robotically. Each person plans differently and throughout your teacher training you will develop the planning style that suits you best.

When planning make sure you plan the Learning Objective first - it is very tempting to plan the activities for the lesson first - but there is often little point in doing an activity if it doesn't contribute to the learning objective. Planning the learning objective first will help ensure that all the activities in your lesson are relevant and will help the children achieve the objectives for the lesson.

How much detail do you need to include?

You plan needs to have enough detail in it to *Enable YOU to teach the lesson* - I know it sounds simple but you need to make sure you know what is going on in the lesson - make sure there is enough detail in the plan to allow this - the shorthand you thought of last night might not mean anything to you in the morning! You also need enough detail to *Enable your additional adults to support you* - If you have any additional adults in the lesson, make sure your plan contains enough detail and is clear enough so that they are able to support you effectively. Finally, you also need to make sure your plans *Show your training provider you can plan* - There is no escaping it - sometimes you are going to have to put extra detail in your plan so that your tutor or mentor can clearly see what was planned to happen in a lesson. You also need to make sure that all your plans include all the things your training provider asks for in your plans.

How long will planning take?

Again this is down to the individual - but expect to spend considerable amounts of time planning each lesson at the start of your training (3 hours for a 1 hour lesson is certainly not unheard of!), but as you gain more experience in teaching and planning, your planning time will decrease.

How do you teach from a plan?

Try not to teach physically holding the plan - by all means have the plan out so you are able to refer to it, but nervously holding your plan in front of you when teaching can give the wrong impression to the children!

You should avoid at all costs using the plan as a 'script' - don't be a slave to your plan. Adapt your plan and even throw the plan out the window (although probably not literally) if needed - you need to respond to the lesson as it happens. Your plan is a guide - just because you have planned it doesn't mean it has to happen - **being able to adapt your lesson 'on the go' is an essential skill.**

#pgcetips on.... Planning and Resources

Carefully check spellings on resources you have created. @mathsatschool

Having a mental block when planning? Try taking a break - stand up and do some ironing / brain free chores then note ideas down.   @tjoo7

RT @mathsatschool: Try to produce a simple resource(s) for your dept that will still be used after you've gone (a small legacy?)
@ mathteachr

Steal ideas! If you see something that you like use it yourself or adapt it. You don't need to reinvent the wheel from scratch.   @ClaireLotriet

Remember ppt is only 1 tool, NOT The Best Tool in the World ever.
@chris_1974

Spend the time you have now creating resources - laminate or print card sorts on card not paper so they last for years!   @marketspi

When laminating card sets do some with matt laminating pouches - shiny ones are hard for visually impaired students to read   @Caro_lann

Even More #pgcetips on....
Planning and Resources

Lessons: always have differentiation for low ability and "fun" extension for high ability. Kids finish get bored mess around.   @Rantingteacher

A lifesaver for me was to do Smartboard slides in the morning rather than spending hours every evening.   @Andrekabu

Don't rely on someone else's plan; adopt and innovate works every time
@2SimpleAnt

Don't plan what you are going to do plan what the children are going to do.   @chris_1974

Learning goals first, activity second. Make the activity fit the goals as too often the activity is put first.@chris_1974

Never try to pick up & use someone else's lesson - you should always adapt to your style / class.   @chris_1974

Involve students in planning the next lesson - what do you want to learn tomorrow?   @mrgpg

Yet more #pgcetips on.... Planning and Resources

Plan in afl throughout the lesson. Plan your key questions of named students.   @mrgpg

Lesson plans aren't cast in stone - keep you mind open as kids often go off on a tangent and that's fine! @ Vickiesheridan

Be savvy with your lesson plans - you're probably doing lots of great things but not noting them on the all-hallowed LP and SOW.
@morphosaurus

When teaching a difficult concept like Spearman's Rank Correlation consider using a fun example like Krispy Kreme doughnuts.
@Morphosaurus

Planning to use IT? NEVER assume that the students can access the resource you want them to use - check a student account 1st   @smckane

Share your ideas and resources with your placement school - they will help you to improve them   @shellbelle21

As a teacher you could work 24 hours a day 365 days a year and still have work to do - Know when to stop planning.   @shellbelle21

The Final #pgcetips on.... Planning and Resoruces

Making resources is time-consuming; invest in your future by making them sturdy and re-useable. Always save templates!   @wizenedcrone

Have 5min fillers handy for starting lesson/ gaps/etc - rebus sudoku riddles - fun brainbenders to settle and focus @katemreid

Have some quick and easy plenaries up your sleeve for when other parts over-run.   @stormfilled

Plan well but don't worry if you don't follow it exactly sometimes it's more about the journey than the destination   @missbrownsword

talk to students about what works for them.   @graemesmith1978

Use Post-it notes to note down quick observations and stick to your planning. The point is do it immediately or you'll forget.   @OhLottie

Remember back to how you felt on your own favourite times as a learner. Work on ways to recreate that for your students. @Magsamond

Your Teaching Style

By Oliver Quinlian

Despite having a National Curriculum in the UK, specifying what all pupils need to be taught, young people still have a huge variety of experiences of learning. Some of this is down to resources, some of it is down to the classes they end up in, but much of it is about the different styles adopted by the vast array of people in the teaching profession.

So what is a teaching style and how do you develop your own? I would argue that your teaching style is basically how you relate what you are doing to your general philosophy of why you are doing the job in the first place. If you are a secondary teacher with a wayward past who took up teaching teenagers so they would have a chance not to repeat your mistakes, that will influence a certain style. If you are a lover of academia who wants to share this thirst for knowledge in a certain subject to those students who think similarly, you will have a different style. If you are a caring person who wants to support young children from difficult backgrounds, this is going to influence another very different style of teaching.

All of these people will have huge strengths as a result of their reasons for teaching, but they will all potentially have huge gaps in their ability to cater for all their students; knowing your style is about knowing what makes you tick, and how you can leverage or adjust that to provide the best opportunities for your students.

Some people may think they couldn't possibly come up with a philosophy of teaching until they have been teaching for years, let alone before they have set foot in a class. Naturally you don't feel like an expert yet, but you don't have to be trained to engage with the things that are important because education is one of the most universal experiences in our society. Your philosophy will be tested, and will be adapted, but if you have one in the first place you can consciously look at where you fit in the profession and what you might need to develop.

When you are planning an activity for your students, think at every stage 'Why am I doing it like this?' If you believe you should be producing independent learners, then ask yourself if setting highly structured worksheets is going to do that. If you believe students should be confident communicators, then there may be better ways to achieve that than insisting that they have to individually record something in their books for every lesson. If you keep asking yourself this question, and relating it to your bigger ideas about what education should be, then you will develop a style all your own, a style which reflects your strengths as a person. Just because you have one style does not mean that you cannot learn from and be influenced by people of different styles. In fact it is essential; as I mentioned earlier, all styles will have weaknesses that don't best cater for all your different students.

Personally I teach from the direction of being very child led, focused on stages of development and listening to what directions pupils st*ant to take. However, I am always really impressed when I observe lessons by very assertive, objective driven teachers. I admire the skills they use to keep a class so focused on a specific thing until it is mastered, and I admire the techniques they use to organise and manage a large number of children and keep them on task. I will never be like that; it doesn't fit into my philosophy to be so didactic, but I certainly benefit from learning those skills to drive a whole class forward in the most efficient way possible. There are also some children who learn best through structure, and if I don't develop the potential to do that into my style then I am potentially failing those particular children.

So think about it, what do you believe in? If you can think consciously about it and relate what you plan back to it, you can start to develop your own style of teaching. There is much to learn from others, but thinking about your own style will set you apart and make sure you are making the most of your strengths, consciously addressing your weaker areas, and providing the students you teach with what you really believe are the best educational chances.

#pgcetips on.... Your Teaching Style

Confidence - there's no difference between someone who IS confident and someone who ACTS confident learn how to appear confident @missbrownsword

enjoy what you do   @raff31

Do it your way   @Rseddon

Be directive influential caring and actively engaged in the passion of teaching and learning   @colport

Don't try to run before you can walk. Your enthusiasm is most welcome, but learn the basics and practice them all the time.   @Mrplume

Be willing to be totally reflective. If something doesn't work out as planned, know that it's ok but learn from it. @ClaireLotriet

Chop one red onion- teachers as 'curriculum makers', your approach to planning and teaching.
by *Alan Parkinson*

Last week, I was making a shepherd's pie, following a recipe in a cookbook. I came to the instruction "Chop one red onion finely", and went to the fridge. There was no red onion, so I picked up my car keys and went to get fish and chips instead...

... Of course, I didn't... I changed the recipe from the one in the cookbook. I used – get this – a shallot instead, and I chopped it coarsely... I also substituted balsamic vinegar for Worcestershire sauce, a bouillon cube for Oxo, red Leicester for Cheddar cheese and some passata for tomato puree... Guess what, it still turned out to be a shepherd's pie... and quite a tasty one...

OK, so what has this got to do with your PGCE placement ? Well... in your first few weeks of your placement you will, if you're lucky be handed some schemes of work which will vary tremendously in the level of detail, mapping of PLTS, timings, resource lists, assessment outcomes, literacy mapping, differentiation opportunities, and a long list of other things. This may well be tied closely to a particular textbook as the key resource to be handed out and opened to a particular page. (I hope this doesn't happen too often when you get to your school...) This is the 'recipe' that you may be asked to follow... I would say that, at the earliest opportunity you should "vary the recipe" to suit your tastes. If the students are happily discussing the results of their group work, don't call a halt just because the lesson plan says you should... go with the flow... vary the tasks. Discuss your reasons for doing this with your mentor, and reflect on the results... No apologies for using the diagram below, which is geographical in context, but can of course be used in any subject. It is what we call "living geography" or "curriculum making"..

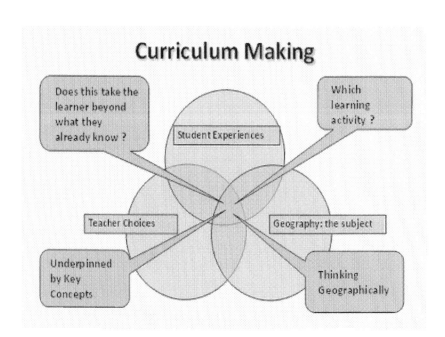

Curriculum making is defined as: "the creation of interesting, engaging and challenging educational experiences which draw upon teacher knowledge and skills, the experiences of students and the valuable subject resource that is geography." The missing ingredient in the lesson plans that you have been given may well be the students' experiences. These can feed into the lesson planning if they are allowed to. Also think about the opportunities that have been provided for students to think geographically. One thing that we have seen time and time again when reading through submissions for our Quality Mark, is that exciting lessons lead to a dramatic reduction in negative classroom behaviours. As you gain confidence, you might try going a little further away from the recipe. You might also discover that the original recipe was the best, and your slight changes didn't actually improve the end result. Some recipes are 'classic' after all... At the end of the lesson, the students will have hopefully progressed a little further in their development as geographers and can begin to articulate this. A final helpful aspect of using my analogy... As I was cooking the pie, I tasted it, and I thought it was quite good... The true test came, of course, when the people I was making it for tasted it. You might have what you think is the best lesson ever, but it needs to be tested with some consumers with 'discerning' tastes. Think about this as being your 'formative assessment'.

A final pie-related metaphor... if all you had to eat was shepherd's pie every day, you'd get a bit fed up of it. Don't overuse any particular technique, resource or pedagogical approach. The phrase 'death by worksheet' is just as likely to have been replaced with 'death by mystery/YouTube clip/IWB drag and drop' etc.

So whether your teaching style is a bit Heston Blumenthal (experimental, wacky, creative ??), Delia Smith (insert appropriate metaphors here) or Jamie Oliver (ditto) have fun, keep tasting as you go, and remember that you don't have to buy the most expensive ingredients to end up with a tasty meal. Bon appétit !

References

http://www.geographyteachingtoday.org.uk/curriculum-making/introduction/ - Curriculum making
http://geography.org.uk/projects/makinggeographyhappen/ - some recipes to follow http://livinggeography.blogspot.com
– the author's main blog... http://geography.org.uk/Journals/Journals.asp?articleID=719 – an article for 'Geography' written by the author on food as a context for learning....

Alan Parkinson Secondary Curriculum Development Leader Geographical Association http://www.geography.org.uk

Managing additional adults.

Additional adults (Teaching Assistants (TAs), Learning Support Assistants (LSAs), parent helpers etc!) are without a doubt the most valuable resource you will have in a lesson. In most primary schools you should find you have at least one teaching assistant for at least some of your lessons (often TAs work mornings only.) In secondary schools there is far more variation in the amount of TA support you will have.

Whilst additional adults are valuable, it's important to remember they are not teachers and therefore there are limits to what you can ask them to do - working with and leading a small group is perfectly acceptable but asking them to teach the whole class is not! Whilst they are unlikely to just sit doing nothing during a lesson, you will get the most out of their support if you actively plan them into the lesson (plan for your TA to work with a specific group(s) or have a specific role).

Communicating with your additional adults is key to maximizing their support. However, due to the ways TAs are generally paid and their working hours, your TA may not arrive in lesson until the children do (or even after the children) so it is unlikely you will have time to run through each lesson with them beforehand. Your class teacher/mentor will probably have a system in place to communicate with your additional adults and you should try to use this to begin with. Many teachers find keeping a notebook in which they write messages/instructions to their TA useful, and TAs will always appreciate being given a copy of your lesson plans! Communication is also key so that you present a 'united front' to the children.

Many teaching assistants are '1-1' TAs – they are 'attached' to a child who has an educational needs statement (put simply, this is the way many schools can afford to have TAs). However, often 1-1 TAs will be able to help 'generally' in the class as well as support their 1-1, but you need to bear this in mind when you are planning them into your lessons, as their 1-1 support will have to take priority over any 'general' tasks in the lesson.

Your TA can also be a vital source of information - they know the children in your class. TAs have also been involved in countless lessons and will know where resources etc can be found in the school - make sure you utilise this knowledge!

Above all, make sure you treat your TA with respect - they do an amazing job for very little money!

Originally Posted:-08/03/2010
Blog Address:- classroomtales.com
Blogger:- Tim Handley

The Hero in My Classroom

There have been quite a few articles over the past week or so, drawing attention to the un-sung heroes of education.

This got me thinking about my un-sung heros and more specifically reflecting on the amazing Teaching assistant's that I have had the absolute pleasure of working with so far during my placements!

You see, I've come to the conclusion that I simply think that teaching assistants are one of the most invaluable 'resources' in the classroom! Whilst I'm sure I could teach without them, I know for certain they make life in the classrooms I teach in much better and also allow me to do things that I prehaps wouldn't have been able to do without the support of a teaching assistant.

The teaching assistants in my current class are a great example of what I think teaching assistants 'should' be like. They are responsive, take great pleasure and delight in their work, are amazing working with children and are always happy and keen to help. We have a 1-1 TA in the class, but she is always happy to help with general class things when she can which is amazing!!

It always makes me smile when I see one of my TA's working with her 1-1 – as she is simply so wonderful with him (I guess that's down to working with him for coming up to 2 years but still- it's amazing to watch!) and I do think that TA's (especially 1-1's) have the potential to build up a stronger relationship with the children than the teacher does (or definitely than a PGCE student on placement does!) as they are often with the same class/children through the school etc...

I am also lucky as I think I have a great working relationships with all the teaching assistants who help in my class. This has a flip side though- it's being quite difficult this placement for me to evidence a point from my action plan of 'managing teaching assistant support effectively'- I don't feel like I have to manage my TA support- yes they are often planned into my plans (and they get copies of the plans- when I remember(!!)) so that they have assigned groups to work with, and yes, I ask them to help out with observational assessments etc- but I defiantly don't feel like I have to explicitly manage their support! I also value my teaching assistants advice, as I recognise that they know the class better than I do (as much as I try!) and things seem different when your not at the front teaching. My TA's are also great at listening, and will often simply listen to me and reassure me(!).

Sadly, I know that some people on my course have experienced completely the opposite with the teaching assistants they have come across. I have heard stories of teaching assistants simply being rude, nasty and unprofessional to PGCE students and taking the view that they know better than the PGCE student and telling the student that in front of the class! Luckily I think this type of response/behaviour is relatively rare but it is still shocking to me that it happens!

I've been thinking about why the TA's in my School A may be particularly amazing! I've come to the conclusion that the fact that my school A is a small, rural school with a great sense of community defiantly helps! There are only 6 TA's in the school (with 5 teachers) so everyone knows each other and importantly knows how each other works and what help they find most useful etc! It also means I have 2 pretty much constant TA's (with no setting etc to switch teaching assistants around!) so they have gotten to really know me and my teaching partner well too!

It does shook me how little TA's get paid! For all the hard work and dedication they put in, they get rewarded very little financially which shows me what a special type of person TA's really are!

TH

#pgcetips on.... Teaching Assitants

Don't forget to share your lesson plans with TA/INA support. We can support you and the children best that way!   @TAtoTeacher

Treat TA with respect! Explain what you would like done. Ask for & Listen to their input. Be clear.   @Ebd35

Working with a TA is like good co-parenting; show a united front regarding behaviour expectations and reward systems! @TAtoTeacher

Have notebook for communication with TA if time2talk a prob Give them an area that's theirs in class so they belong @ebd35

Ask your TA for advice & support. We've seen lots of teaching practice and we know where lots of useful resources are too!   @TatoTeacher

Having been a TA for the past 2 years learn what skills they have and USE them! You are a team work like one   @imaverickjr

Support your TA's professional development - you can share learning experiences. @TAtoTeacher

Assessment

By Nikki Davies

What is it?

Put simply, assessment is how you find out whether the students have learnt what you wanted them to learn or not. Done well, it's also the way to move them on in their learning. Assessment can take many forms, from the praise and feedback you give to children during the course of a lesson, to the formal tests carried out at the end of key stages.

Step one: Know what you're assessing

Every lesson you teach will have a learning objective. Remember to focus on that when you're assessing. It's really useful to come up with "success criteria" with the children, so that they take ownership of the learning.

For example, if you are learning to write instructions, together you might come up with 3 success criteria:

1)   Use imperative verbs
2)   Use adverbs
3)   Use bullet points or numbers

When you assess this piece of work, you then focus on whether the children have achieved these three targets.

Formative assessment

Formative assessment is assessment that's carried out day to day to give children feedback on their learning. This includes what is known as AfL or "Assessment for Learning".
We can probably all remember the teachers who would just tick your work and give comments such as "VG" or "SEE ME!" – but you will do much better than that!

Verbal feedback

This is the first port of call for formative assessment. Praise and comments about their work are really important to children, and verbal feedback will also be your main way of giving feedback to children in KS1. When giving feedback, remember to be specific.
Instead of saying "What a lovely picture!" – which is vague and can sound insincere -
Say: "I really like the way you've mixed that shade of blue."

2 Stars and a Wish

This is a great way to mark against success criteria. It involves writing 2 comments about what children have done well, and 1 comment about how they could improve it.
* You have used bullet points really well
* You chose a great range of imperative verbs
W Could you try to add a few adverbs?

If you can, try to give a few minutes at the start of the next lesson so the children can read your comments and act on the wish. In my example above, the child would go through their work and add in the adverbs. This is then moving them forward in their learning and helping them onto the next step. This marking technique is very time intensive, however, so you should probably try to do it no more than a few times a week.

Self and Peer Assessment

Again, this helps the children to take ownership of their own assessment. If 2 stars and a wish is part of your school policy, the children should already be familiar with it – if not, you will have to model it a few times first. They should soon be confident with giving a partner or themselves 2 stars and a wish. In my experience, they love having this responsibility and I have never seen it used inappropriately – in fact, they sometimes pick up on things I have missed! It's a great way of getting them to look at their own work and evaluate it. You can also use "marking ladders" for this, which are available on the internet for many genres of writing.

A really quick and effective method for self assessment is to use traffic lights. The children simply mark their work with a small green, yellow or red circle to show how well they feel they have achieved the learning objective. A colleague of mine also asks children to write R, Y, or G on their mini whiteboards just before starting work to show how confident they feel. This helps him target the children who will need help most during that lesson. Another way of getting immediate feedback is to ask for "thumbs up or down".

Written feedback

When marking work, sometimes you are so busy that you have to make do with a "Well done". When you have time, though, it's great to follow the same principles as with verbal feedback. A short sentence such as "Great use of similes" doesn't take too long and is much more meaningful to the child.

Recording

You will need to come up with a way of recording that works for you. You will probably be asked to keep records of what children have achieved in each lesson.
As I said earlier, remember to stay focused on those learning objectives. What did you want the children to learn, and who has learnt it?

A simple way is to start with a class list with lots of room at the top to write in the objectives. This could be a printed list or you could make up a simple spreadsheet. (Remember to be aware of confidentiality issues. I just used initials of the children rather than full names.)

		Use bullet points	Imperative verbs	Use adverbs						
R	A									
K	B									
N	B									
E	B									
K	C	Abs	Abs	Abs						

Here's my example. This is a basic "traffic light" system. As you can see, RA has really got the hang of bullet points and imperative verbs, but didn't use any adverbs.

KB used a few bullet points but didn't quite get it. He was very good at the other two objectives, though. NB had no problems. EB has struggled with this, as you can see, and will need more help next time. KC was off so missed all this work.

This system will help you to see how to target your support in the next lesson and who is ready to move on. Your tutors should also like it as it shows evidence of your assessment. It's probably a good idea to have your record sheet next to you as you mark so you can get both jobs done at once.

Summative Assessment

Summative assessment is the more formal, end-of-year type tests that "sum up" the learning so far. Some schools carry out tests each half term, others termly, and others only do the QCA tests (SATS) during the summer term. You will not be asked to administer these tests, but if you get the chance it's really useful to sit in on a marking session, particularly in the writing tests.

APP

APP – Assessing Pupils' Progress – is a form of diagnostic assessment that is being considered as a replacement for QCA tests. Time will tell whether the present government decide to stick with it or not!

APP works with a focus group of 3 children working at different levels in the class. You select a sheet based on the level the chosen pupil is currently working at and the one they're aiming for – your placement teacher will help you with this. The sheet lists all the different skills and targets the child needs to achieve in order to attain that level. You then need to find evidence in the child's work of them achieving this target without support. You can then highlight that as "achieved". The "gaps" will show you what you need to focus on in your teaching.

Your placement teacher will give you help with this, but if you get stuck or want to know more, example standards files are found here:
http://nationalstrategies.standards.dcsf.gov.uk/search/primary/results/nav:45920

Near the bottom of this page is a glossary to help you understand what the APP writing targets actually mean:
http://schools.norfolk.gov.uk/index.cfm?s=1&m=1144&p=767,index

Remember

It can be quite a daunting prospect, but try to keep up with your marking and assessment – little and often is the key. Always keep in mind that the assessment you do should be useful and meaningful for both you and the children.

#pgcetips on.... Assessment

Assessment is key driver for standards , Student motivation and a key driver for good/outstanding lessons under OFSTED framework @dan_bowen

Use a code as a quick tool to assess against L.I e.g. full triangle= met L.I 2 sides = partially met 1 side = hasn't yet met. @OhLottie

Try to sit down with an experienced teacher to level some work with. Really helpful to see how other people do it.   @Oliverquinlan

Rather than the Red Pen Of Doom try the Pink Pen Of Mild Peril - it looks less like blood when you hand the work back.   @Morphosaurus

Stay on top of marking student work. Not doing so can result in a more stress filled week.   @4goggas

No one ever does enough self-assessment and peer-assessment exercises. Kids get more out of it and you'll get breathing space. @Morphosaurus

Students - do not neglect to mark the work you set the pupils! @rantingteacher

Don't put off innovation
by Oliver Quinlan

"If you do what you've always done, you'll get what you've always gotten."
Anthony Robbins

When I was completing my PGCE we had a number of guest lectures from an expert on synthetic phonics. The University, quite rightly, deemed this to be very important as none of us had been taught to read using this method, and were entirely unfamiliar with it. I was flabbergasted by the number of fellow students who expressed the opinion that this method of teaching backed up by scientific research was 'a load of rubbish'. Their reason? They never learned to read using such a 'convoluted' method, and they had 'turned out all right'.

At the time this surprised me, but I find it is actually quite a common reaction when people are faced with new ways of doing things in the classroom. It is a dangerous point of view because it shows an implicit assumption that the world we are educating children for is the same as the one we were educated for. It is not. I am a young teacher, but in the 15 years since I was at primary school I have gone from having one computer for 30 children in my class, to carrying in my pocket a computer 1000 times more powerful that is constantly connected to the Internet. That changes things. A lot.

A world of constant, instant connection both to others and to factual knowledge requires hugely different skills. A class of children educated for a world of the authoritative but quickly outdated knowledge contained in printed books are not being prepared for navigating the immediate, but often dubiously reliable flow of information on the Internet. A class of children given no experience of publishing to a wide audience are liable to make some massive gaffes when they discover the freedom to do so as teenagers and vent ill-considered opinions to the entire world. A class of children treated by their teacher as vessels to be filled with factual knowledge must feel short changed when they realise they can access all this knowledge and more with a few taps of the touchscreen in their pocket. My class have realised that already. They are 8.

Education needs to change, as it is quickly becoming irrelevant to the world that today's children live in. As teachers, we may be stuck in the past but these children are not, and if we don't keep up we will quickly become irrelevant too.

So, you may be wondering what a 'mere' PGCE student can do about all this. My answer is recognise that education needs to change to match this new world, and make that change now. You will come across many people that urge you to 'concentrate on the basics', to observe experienced teachers and mimic what they do, and to sort out your day to day practice before trying something different. To a certain extent this is true, there are a lot of basics to learn and a lot of great people to use as examples, but you needn't be the same as them. After all, most of them trained in a time that is ancient history to the children they are teaching.

You will never be more eager to try things out, you will never be less jaded about experimenting, and you will never have the same spark to innovate as you do when you first start. You might not know some of the 'basics', the ways things have always been done, but that puts you in an excellent position to look at things in terms of what is most effective rather than what has become habit. You aren't limited by the preconceptions that experienced teachers have, so you have the perfect opportunity to come up with new ideas. Seize it.

If things go wrong you have the luxury of being a beginner, you won't be the first PGCE student to do a failure of a lesson, people will forgive you. If you make some colossal mistakes, then you will be out of there in a few weeks anyway and class teachers expect trainees to be less than perfect. Granted, you might need to rein yourself in a bit if you have an important observation coming up, or if your experimenting is losing you the respect of colleagues and pupils, but you will never have a better time to take some risks and try some new things.

If you think you can't make a difference as an inexperienced teacher, you are wrong. Whilst completing his PGCE Tim Handley, the editor of this book, started a blog of his ideas and reflections. By the time he had got his QTS certificate it had been viewed nearly 13,000 times. That is 13,000 expressions of interest in his innovative lesson ideas. By the end of my NQT year I had been invited to present at the headquarters of Internet giant Google, and advise my local authority on embedding technology in the classroom. You can make a difference, if you make a commitment to do so from the start.

Don't put off innovation. If you go into a placement and decide to do everything in the same way that your experienced class teacher does then you are already stuck in someone else's rut. If you put ideas aside and tell yourself you will innovate next year it will never happen. Your NQT year has many more pressures not to innovate, such as full responsibility for achievement and results. If you start as you mean to go on you will always be an innovative teacher, you will always be receptive to change and will always keep yourself relevant and meaningful to your pupils and the world they are growing up into.

Isn't that what they deserve?

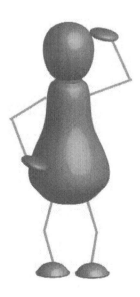

#pgcetips on.... *Trying New Things*

Don't be afraid to try new things (esp. tech) but expect to come up for criticism as some teachers are afraid of change @squiggle7

After-school clubs are a great place to try out activity ideas before using them in class. If there isn't one you could start one   @STEMclubs

Leave your own school experience behind and look with fresh eyes. Education has probably changed a lot since you were last in it!
@Lauradoggett

Don't be afraid to try things for yourself. Risk taking is v. valuable and is a great thing to pass on to pupils   @elativism

If you change your mind about a lesson just before or even during then change the lesson. Off the cuff nearly always pays off   @Rseddon

Don't be scared of using current tech in lessons. Frame homeworks around it - write a Facebook profile for the elements etc.   @smckane

Be confident in yourself your ideas and your skills at every level. This will show through in your teaching   @relativism

#pgcetips on.... Looking after yourself!

Drink lots of water to try and save your voice.   @Cloudlilly

Don't carry on regardless if you are ill or you'll only be ill for longer. And you will get ill.   @squiggle7

Keep a bottle of antibacterial hand gel and pack of baby wipes close by at all times!   @ClaireLotriet

'Timetable' some social activities and make sure you take some exercise as it's easy to feel overwhelmed with new responsibilities   @pastures-greener

Wash your hands before you eat anything - children have a LOT of germs! @squiggle7

Don't become too bogged down in it: easy to lose perspective. Have at least 1 fun thing planned each wknd. You'll be better for it @rantingteacher

...tachers don't always practise what we preach... We should take a leaf out of our own tips and stop stressing every weekend! @rantingteacher

Your 'I Can't do this' Moment

At some point during the PGCE year (probably during a placement), you will almost definitely have a period where you simply think 'I can't do this'. You will probably think that you stand no chance of becoming a teacher or passing the course.

What triggers these moments obviously varies - it could be a lesson, day or week of teaching that you think hasn't gone well, you may have made what you consider to be a catastrophic 'mistake', an observation may not have gone as well as you hoped or a comment made by someone may have unsettled you.

But don't panic - practically everyone has had these moments - especially during the PGCE year! When you are having an 'argghh' moment, try to remember a few things:-

•Remember you are not expected to be perfect - you are a trainee teacher and no-one (apart from you!) expects your lessons to be perfect and all singing and all dancing!
•Teachers learn constantly - it's part and parcel of the profession!
•Remember that even teachers with 30+ years experience in the classroom still have 'off' lessons, day and weeks and that everyone makes 'mistakes'.
•You naturally are self critical - things often seem much worse 'from the front'
•You are still on your training course - therefore your training provider must have confidence that you can do it!
•What you perceive to be a 'bad' observation can be useful! You will learn and have the support and guidance of the person observing you.
•Remember all observations will also be full of positive things that you have done well - make sure you read these and don't just focus on the 'improvements' or 'targets'.

Most importantly, when you are having one of these 'arghh' moments, don't suffer in silence. Tell others how you are feeling. You will probably have been given lots contact details (including home/mobile numbers) for your university tutor - if you are having one of these moments, use them! Your tutor at university is there to support you and they really won't mind! Having one (or more) of these moments is not a weakness - your training provider will not cast judgment on you for it - all they will want to do is support you!

If it's a lesson, day or week that's made you feel like this, then try to do some good quality reflections and evaluations - making sure you pick out the positive points as well! It can also be helpful to take a break - try to make sure you give yourself an evening, or even better, a weekend, where you can 'switch off' slightly from the PGCE - do something that you enjoy and treat yourself!

Your mentor at school is also a valuable source of support and re-assurance - after all, they will probably have seen you teach more than anyone else! Other members of staff at your placement school will almost always be willing to help - especially those who are recently qualified. You may also want to speak to fellow students who are always a fantastic source of support!

But whatever you do - don't give up - you will emerge from an 'arghhh' moment stronger!

My PGCE Tips

There is one thing that strikes me, when I read other PGCE-related posts... something that I just don't really understand or agree with. Everyone constantly harps on about how stressful it is.

I'm in a lucky position in that I don't get stressed easily. I have the mindset that it's all going to be alright in the end. There is always a light at the end of the tunnel and there's always somewhere to run to for help (more so than ever on the PGCE course).

But I'd be lying if I said I didn't get stressed this year. There were three real key moments where I just broke down. However, I learnt things from those dark times, so they probably did me a whole lotta good.

The first tearful time, was brought on by my personal circumstances. In September I not only started a PGCE course, I also moved to London to live with complete strangers. As a result, I had the stress of making friends and setting up a support network, on top of the PGCE workload. A month or so into the course I realised how exhausted I was, and it wasn't necessarily from the course. I realised I was exhausted from being a nice, smiling, everyone's best friend, instead of being myself and getting on with things.

So, tip number one: Don't panic about making friends on the course. Even if you're at university in your sleepy home town and you don't think you need any extra friends, you'll still feel the pressure to fit in and make friends. But they'll come, in time. You're on such an intense course so close bonds with course-mates are inevitable.

The second little breakdown I had was when I took my teaching practice to France. Again, it's not a typical PGCE situation, and I, again, made things hard for myself. With a D in A-Level French, there was no way I should have been allowed to teach children in a completely foreign language. I do regret it slightly... but I also feel the university should have flagged up my poor language skills and recommended I stayed in the UK. But anyway.

I went to France, I sat at the back of a French classroom and I felt it all happening around me. I had no idea what was going on; the situation and language were completely alien to me. I went home and cried my eyes out. I spoke to my tutor in England and told him I didn't think I'd be able to cope, but the support just wasn't there (and lead to me making a formal complaint to the university). Despite my mini-breakdown, I got on with it. I became glued to my dual language dictionary and the children were forced to speak very slowly to me. But I did it. I taught maths, geography, history etc... in French. The key message on my end of practice observation: Rosie taught well despite barely adequate French.

So, tip number 2: Just get on with it. By all means, ask for help, but at the end of the day you need to just stop worrying and stop finding it stressful. I wasn't going to learn French over-night, and you're not going to control the behaviour of an unruly class over-night. But you're there to learn and improve, and the moment you stop stressing is the moment any situation (no matter how petrifying) becomes worthwhile.

The third and final breakdown was the most impressive. I had my I can't do this moment that every trainee teacher has. Again, my situation was slightly abnormal, but I didn't bring it on myself this time. During my final placement, my class teacher went into hospital for an operation. As a result, she was off school for two weeks preceding half term. It was only my third week at the school, but the headteacher made the decision to not call in cover. I was told I'd be taking the class in the teacher's absence. This shouldn't have been the case... I was there to learn, and I wasn't supposed to be teaching the class full-time at that point in my training. But my tutor did nothing about it; he merely assured me that the headteacher felt I was capable. And so that was that... again, I asked for help and was told to just get on with it. So I did.

The actual moment of my breakdown is a complicated story, in which I was denied my planning time so had an absolute panic and didn't have anything to teach the children. I, again, asked for help from various people, but, again, I was given no support. The result was a tearful conversation with my mother who told me to just get on with it. I can honestly say that those two weeks with the class to myself were the best of the whole year. Once I realise that they were mine and I was free to do what I wanted with them (within reason) I settled into it and did it my way.

Tip number three: throw yourself in the deep end. It might not work for everyone, I understand that, but when it comes to taking the class in your final placement I really can't stress how much good it did me to have them all to myself. I know other people on my course never took the class without their teacher being present. Having them completely to myself meant that they were my class. It meant I

had to take over the itty bitty tasks, such as spelling tests and reading records. The silly bits and bobs that, as a trainee you don't even consider. As a trainee you plan your lessons and don't really take the general running of the class into consideration. Trips are planned for you, Sports Day is organised and you're given a job, the milk money is collected without you realising and the parents come to the class teacher with concerns. But it's not real, and it's not going to be like that when I have my own class.

So, although there have been the stressful times, I reckon they've been the times I've done the most learning. I can't understand why there is such a focus on how stressful it is. Surely that just puts a negative spin on it and you're setting yourself up to struggle.

Final tip: It's all about time management. Set yourself working hours and don't work outside them. I never worked at a weekend (except the last few when I was sorting out my Standards folder). The only work I did outside of school was book-marking because I had an hour-long train journey every morning and evening so I had nothing better to do. If you tell yourself you need to get your work done by the time you leave the classroom, you will. You need your free time.From The Blogsphere

#pgcetips to read when you need picking up!

When everything seems to be going wrong try not to worry. that moment happened to everyone. look at how far you've come!   @MarkAMacInnes

Remember you're learning too when things go wrong don't panic. This is when you learn the most so reflect and embrace mistakes.   @relativism

Remember most of what is written about education is waffle and it is what actually happens in children's minds that is important   @thisissimz

Don't despair and rip up your teaching folder if you have a bad lesson. It happens to everyone. Nor if you have a bad day. @lisibo

You'll only discover how flexible you can be when the plan goes wrong but it all goes fine. Don't fear it.   @Stormfilled

The students you're finding difficult will be the same ones that all the other teachers find difficult whatever their experience @mandared

Don't be too hard on yourself it can be too easy to do so but remember we all make mistakes regardless of exp.   @relativism

more #pgcetips to read when you need picking up!

If you have a bad day learn from it and move on. Never be afraid to ask for help and advice. Don't be scared to take risks. @DMcCrory82

Embrace errors as a welcomed learning opportunity for you and the pupils @colport

Ask lots of questions. Ask about strategies for teaching, management, planning. If u don't ask, u don't get. Then ask sum1 else ;) @mister_jim

Don't expect to get everything right to remember everything or to be perfect. Do your best but remember when to call it a day. @Smckane

don't beat yourself up if you get something wrong. You are training to be a teacher you're learning!   @Graemesmith1978

it's good 2 look back at your letter of application every now & then. It shows u at your best & can help u keep that focus @Smichael920

Stick it out even when you're knackered from all the planning & paperwork it's really worth it in the end. Best job in the world!   @mfl_noemie

Nearing the end - Stepping things up

As you approach the end of your course, you will probably find two things which go hand in hand.

•All your assignments and the majority of your university based sessions will be over - this means you have all your time to concentrate on teaching.

•You will be expected to teach for a considerable amount of time and by the end of the course you will probably be teaching a full timetable.
Hopefully by this stage of the course you will be starting to feel confident as a teacher - you will have passed numerous observations and be well on your way to providing evidence that you meet all the QTS standards.

This period of the course can be one of the most enjoyable, but also one of the most demanding. There are a few things you can do to help make the last few weeks fantastic!

•**Ease yourself into full days and full weeks -** You will find yourself being required to teach full days and then full weeks - something which will have been unimaginable just a few months ago! Don't underestimate how exhausting this can be. It's important you ease yourself into this and continue to build up your teaching time gradually so you are able to cope with the demands this brings - don't, for instance, go from teaching 2 hours a day straight into teaching a full week !

•**Make sure you still feel supported -** you will probably find that you will be doing a considerable amount of teaching 'on your own' without your mentor/class teacher present and this can be a great experience. However, don't be afraid to ask for help or for your class teacher/mentor to be present in a particular lesson - they are still there to support you. It is also important that you know where you can find your class teacher/mentor when they are not in the classroom with you.

•**Keep on top of your paperwork -** your training provider will probably still require the same paperwork they did from previous placements and it is really important that you make yourself keep on top of your evaluations etc and don't put them off - the last thing you want is having to write 10 evaluations the night before a visit from your tutor!

•**Keep on top of your assessment -** with increased teaching comes more work that needs to be assessed - make sure you keep on track with your marking - and be sure to make sure you have marked all the work you have set the children before you leave the placement!

•**Keep your classroom organised** - the classroom will probably be more or less 'yours' for these few weeks - make sure it is kept tidy and you know where things are. Your class teacher/mentor will probably be invaluable in helping you develop strategies for this. You should also respect that it still isn't 'your' classroom!

Above all - enjoy the last few weeks - it is an amazing time!

Reflective writing

By Amanda O'Dell

During your teacher training you'll be asked to undertake reflective writing for several different purposes, and it's likely that this style of writing will be new to the majority of trainees. Your reflection will need to happen on two levels: firstly as your personal evaluations of individual lessons, and secondly as an ongoing evaluation of your progress as a teacher and learner throughout your training programme. This reflection will help you to recognise and address areas for development, but it will also play an important role in the support that your tutor and mentor provide and as evidence towards meeting QTS standards. Remember that anything you write you'll need to be able to share, so keep it professional and anonymous.

The process of reflection is something that can be tempting to skip when you're trying to stay on top of things, but it is a vital part of the course and becomes meaningless if you try to go back and piece it together too long after the event. If you don't stop to explore why something is going well or badly, then it's just luck whether things keep going well or you repeat your mistakes, and you haven't got time for that!

Lesson evaluations

Evaluating individual lessons is something that you will be doing mostly for your own benefit soon after teaching each one (although some may be used for evidence later) and it doesn't need to be long-winded – in fact, brief notes will probably help you more. Since every lesson is part of your training programme, this is where you have the chance to make sure that you are indeed learning from every lesson.

You may be provided with a specific format or come up with a structure of your own, but you will need to consider:

What went well about the lesson?
How do you know it went well (what is your evidence)?
What didn't work as well as it could/should have?
What would you change if you taught it again?
How will this lesson inform your planning for the next one?

Reflective diary

More general reflection on your progress is not something that you can undertake usefully after every lesson or even every day, but more likely as a diary that you complete weekly once you've had a chance to distance yourself slightly from the issues raised by individual lessons. It will be useful to you in several ways – to help you consider the progress that you're making and plan your own development; for discussion with your tutor and mentor, showing your engagement with the training programme; and as evidence for some of the QTS standards that might be difficult to meet in other ways.

Exactly how you write this will vary enormously from one teacher to another, but it needs to focus on your development as a teacher rather than simply summarising the issues raised in your lesson evaluations.

It should therefore also include reflection on learning that takes place in university or through your own reading as well as in school. This is probably the most important and effective form of reflection that you will undertake, and it is important that you set aside the time to engage with it effectively. You should reflect on your achievements as well as your difficulties, and explore the reasons that you are making progress or finding difficulties in any particular area. It is then vital that you use this reflection to identify the action that you intend to take next, both to consolidate your achievements and to continue your development.

#pgcetips on... Reflections and Evaluations

No matter how great your lesson is there will always be something you can improve. Don't dwell on the negatives
@missbrownsword

You will have bad days no matter how hard you try. Remember that everyone has them it's probably nothing you did!
@MrsGaskell27

Take time to evaluate your own lessons-record gd and bd aspects-keep a record of evals and use them to inform future planning   @Sport_ed

Take time to reflect on your practice and remember why you chose this profession.
@Smichael920

Try to start a reflective diary before you start the course what you want out of it what your worried about etc   @andyjb

Observations and Assessment of Teaching

Love them (or more likely) loathe them, observations of your teaching are part and parcel of any teacher training course.

There is no hiding the fact that you will probably dread the prospect of your observations - but there is no escaping them. After all, training providers can only assess so much on paper, and many of the QTS standards can only be demonstrated by being observed teaching. Observations are not necessarily the most pleasant of experiences but the following tips may help minimise the stress and anxiety!

Make sure the lesson is well planned - sounds obvious, but make sure you have planned the lesson in depth and that you have included everything your training provider expects to see in your plans.

Make sure everything is prepared for the lesson well in advance - this includes any photocopying and your IWB files etc. Also make sure you have copies of your lesson plan and any resources ready to give to your observer.

Let someone else check your plans - if you are being observed by your university tutor your class teacher will often be more than happy to check over your plans for you. If it's your class teacher/mentor observing you, why not ask another member of staff who knows the class or another student to have a look over them for you?

Get your folder ready - your observer will probably want to look through your teaching practice file/folder - make sure it's in order and up to date and it's one less thing for you to worry about.

Try to make sure you arrange for your advisor to be there when the children arrive. If you are teaching first thing, why not see if your observer can be there from the start of the school day so that you can register the class, complete your morning routines and then go straight into your lesson without the disruption of a 'stranger' coming into the class. Your observer will only formally observe your lesson and can be reading your paperwork etc whilst you are registering the class.

Decide where you'd like your observer to sit - somewhere that isn't in direct line of sight when you are at the front teaching is normally best, but bear in mind they will benefit from seeing the board too!

Introduce your observer - obviously only relevant for external advisors. In primary, check with your observer first, but it can help to introduce them by their first name. Something like "You may have notice we have a special visitor in the room, this is Eleanor and she's one of my friends from university who has come to see how great you are at [insert subject here]" often works well.

Don't be afraid to deviate from your plan - you observer is not assessing how well you can stick to a plan, but how well you can teach. Your observer will be pleased to see you can adapt your lesson to the learners' needs (but don't try to 'plan' opportunities for you to deviate from your plan!)

Ignore your observer(!) - remember you are still teaching the class - be careful not to 'teach' to the observer and avoid constantly looking at them.

Don't be worried if your observer starts to walk around the room - they are likely to do this, and yes, sod's law says they are most likely to go and talk to the one student you'd rather them not talk to - but don't worry about this, your class will very rarely let you down and your observer will go on the whole lesson rather than the comment of one child!

Remember your observer is not trying to 'catch you out' - they are there to find evidence of which QTS standards you meet - not find evidence of those that you don't. Your observer is there to support you in your development as a teacher.

Make sure you are not teaching the lesson after your observation - your observer will often need this time to feed back to you and in any case you will have earned a rest!

Listen to the feedback and take it all on board.

Don't just focus on the negatives - your observer will always state plenty of positive points about the lesson.

If you have any questions - ask them! Likewise, if you feel you need help in a particular area, ask for it - your observer will be more than happy to help you and it is not a sign of weakness!

A 'bad' observation is not the end of the world - 'bad' lesson observations happen - and you are unlikely to escape your training without a lesson observation that you felt went terribly!! Try to not let it knock your confidence. Also remember what you perceive to be 'bad' probably really wasn't that 'bad' at all.

Your observer will always find areas for improvement - after all no one is perfect and even 'outstanding' lessons can be improved in some small way.

#pgcetips on.... Observations

Stick with it. I wept head in hands after 1 lesson obs. Tutor persuaded me to stick with it. Never looked back @dughall

Remember that lesson obs differs to everyday lesson: no point in silent reading or copying from board (I've seen it done!!) @rantingteacher

Deviate from lesson plan if necessary! But say "I had planned to do... but I can see you need to build confidence with... first" @marketspi

The students observe you every lesson. Get feedback from them on what worked / didn't and what they like to do. @Mrgpg

Find out who is observing you & what their interests/specialisms are. Adjust your plan to fit. @Oliverquinlan

When observed don't assume anything in your lesson plans. If you don't write something down you often don't get credit for it. @Oliverquinlan

The best laid plans may change - adapt and deviate away from what you wrote if the class need more time or more explanation @2SimpleAnt

More #pgcetips on.... Observations

Have your planning to hand and don't be frightened to scribble observations on it. Remember it's a working document so use it. @OhLottie

Tutors say they don't like to see neat files- use your plans and annotate them! @tomhenzley

Do not ignore advice given to you after observations   @rantingteacher

When you get feedback remember to listen for the positives it can be too easy to hear development points and miss your strengths   @relativism

Get permission first but get into the habit of taking photos frequently. It's often the best form of evidence. @ClaireLotriet

Remember to introduce your observer to the class- they are a 'stranger' after all! @tomhenzley

No matter how great your lesson is there will always be something you can improve. @tomhenzley

#pgcetips on that made us laugh...

To prove that teachers can be funny(!) here four tweets that didn't fit anywhere else but made us laugh!

""sexylonglegs@email-provider.net"" is unlikely to get the right kind of job interviews" @bill-gibbon

"@billgibbon:"" ""sexy-longlegs@email.net"" unlikely to get right kind of job interviews""(but could get something way more lucrative?)" @tonyparkin

occasionally make your colleagues some #pgtips they will appreciate the favour! @Nstone

don't get #pgcetips confused with #pgtips as drinking lots of tea won't help you pass the course! @AndyRoss75

#pgcetips on.... General Teaching

Ask for help! It's not a sign of weakness but maturity. It's ok to struggles with some or in my case nearly all classes!   @mfl_noemie

Bring to the class/school new ideas and energy   @raff31

Immerse yourself fully in school life. Clubs, meetings, socials Duke of Edinburgh sports etc.   @chris_1974

Be comfortable with admitting mistakes. Don't use the old 'just testing' line.   @ mathsatschool

Get involved with school life as much as possible. Stay for school discos summer fetes etc. If you have time (ha!) start a club.   @Cloudlilly

Get used to darkness. End of Nov is a depressing time. When you leave and return in darkness it gets you down but battle through! @bigtabs88

If you're teamteaching a lesson make sure it is a team effort. It's obvious if one person has done all the work   @lisibo

More General #pgcetips

If you need to speak to a pupil on their own after class do so in plain sight of others or leave the classroom door wide open. @TempleofAnubis

See the year as a whole: explore the connections between theory and practice read /widely/ and be willing to experiment.   @mberry

If you don't know the answer to a pupil question don't make it up. Either look it up for next lesson or get THEM to look it up.   @ Mathsatschool

Don't be too hard on yourself - remember it's a learning process & students take time to get to know you!   @ZoeRoss19

This is a year to be a student and to become a teacher: take an active part in both communities. @Mberry

Try to keep a sense of humour and a smile on your face even at the hardest times. Try to remember that teaching is a privilege @pasturesgreener

After your PGCE keep in touch with your college/uni - the staff often have interesting research ongoing or grants @stevebunce

Even more general #pgcetips

Do one or two duties a week (bus lunch break) with another teacher. This gets you seen by the students and you start networking! @MarkAMacInnes

Listen to experienced colleagues learn from them but don't be scared of ignoring advice and learning from your own mistakes! @nstone

Teaching is lots of hard work but when a student gets it it's the best job in the world. @Baggiepr

This is what you want to do don't forget to have fun along the way. A happy teacher is far more likely to have a happy class @relativism

When a child respond negatively to your efforts there are many reasons. Like everyone children have bad days too. @MarkAMacInnes

Don't be afraid to admit that something isn't working and change tactics pupils will respect u more than if u keep plodding on @relativism

You'll have ups and downs but it's all about focus. Focus on the ups and you'll love your career! :-) @asober

From The Tweeters

What not to do on placement...

To end this section on placements, the Twitterers were asked:-

"What should a Trainee Teacher NOT do on placement?"

Here are their responses!

Never discuss another teacher (esp perceived shortfalls) with pupils. Present a united front which provides consistency.   @TempleofAnubis

Don't tell the class teacher they are doing it wrong (even if they are...)
. . . and to follow on don't tell a class their normal teacher is doing it wrong
@chris_1974

A student should not tell the teacher they know better.   Kid you not!
@Natty08

DON'T ask for advice, receive advice and then completely fail to act upon it.   @TeaKayB

DON'T wander into a lesson having blatantly not prepared and then act all confused about why it all went rump over bumps.   @TeaKayB

Should not arrive late and leave early. Should not make excuses on why they cannot do something! My fave one coming up :) @Natty08

More things not to do on placement...

Should not pretend to faint to get out of obs;--- yes that happened not to me though! @Natty08

Don't turn up to your registration every day with coat already on and bag in hand. It doesn't look great!   @Dailydenouement

Don't let the kids get into class before you! Also don't get behind on paper work the teaching file is important!   @Natty08

Don't take a newspaper to read whilst pupils do a worksheet - doesn't give a good impression...   @lisibo

If a pupil has made the food by hand don't eat it. @Morphosaurus

Try not to fall down stairs on the first day and end up on crutches @Natty08 - that was MY downfall ;o) @lisibo

Finishing the Course

CONGRATULATIONS - you've done it! You've reached the end of your PGCE and are (or will soon be) the proud holder of Qualified Teacher Status!

At the end of the course you will probably feel:-

•**Relieved** – that it's all over and you've got through one of the most difficult years of your teaching career.
•**Pleased** - as you are now a qualified teacher and are officially a member of one of the world's best professions!
•**Bereft** – that you have left behind some great placement classes and some great schools and that you have also left behind a great group of tutors and fellow students.
•**Exhausted** - after all it's been a long year and probably a super busy last few weeks.
•**Anxious** - about what comes next and having your 'own' class.

This section will cover everything you need to know about job hunting (which you will probably start way before you have finished the course) and also give a insight into what lies ahead for you in your NQT year.

Jobs, Applications and Interviews

By Emma Dawson

So, you've survived this far. You are doing this course for one reason only and that is to become a teacher. In order to do that you need to find a job. The area you live in, or want a job in, is going to have an effect on the availability of jobs and the amount of applicants you have to beat. There is a greater demand than supply everywhere, but particularly in the north of the country at the moment (2010). That doesn't mean you won't get a job, just that you have to work harder at making your application stand out from the crowd.

Finding Jobs

First of all, decide what sort of post you are looking for. Full time or part time? Which area of the country - are you willing to look anywhere or do you need to stay in a certain place? Big city school or small village school? There are many places you can look for jobs and not all Local Authorities advertise in the same way. Try jobs.tes.co.uk , www.eteach.com , http://www.epm.co.uk/ , Local Authority websites, the TES newspaper and local newspapers. Some Local Authorities also run a 'pool' system for NQT applicants. Basically, you apply to the 'pool' which is a database for all schools to look at. Schools might see your application and invite you for an interview. Some Local Authorities even guarantee a job from the 'pool' so it's worth looking into.

Applications

Once you've found a few jobs you'd like to apply to the first thing to do is get in contact and arrange a visit (if you can). Some schools won't interview you if you haven't been to visit. If you really can't, make it explicit when you ask for an application form and try to make a telephone appointment to chat to the Headteacher.

It's amazing how much you can tell about a school from visiting and it might put you off a few. Remember though, when you go to visit they may already be making subconscious judgements about you so act professionally, ask questions and seem interested.

Getting the application form right is the most important thing when applying for teaching posts; you've got to make your application stand out from the rest, and the rest could be 50 - 100 other applications - it needs to have the WOW factor. You need to convince the reader that you will be the best person for the job in 2 sides of A4 maximum. Here's a quick list of dos and don'ts:

Do:
Check your spelling and grammar very carefully,
Have someone else proof-read it for you,
Personalise it to the school you are applying to,

Include the school's name in the letter,
Let them know all the skills you have to offer them and how you could apply them,
Make sure you cover all the essential qualities and as many as possible of the desir able qualities in the person specification explicitly,
Address it to the Headteacher personally.

Don't:

Copy phrases from someone else's letter of application, if you both apply they will both end up in the bin,
Send a generic letter to all schools (except if it's for a pool).
Lie, it will come back to bite you in the bum eventually!

Interviews

You've made it through the application stage and you have an interview - congratulations! For most interviews you are likely to be asked to do a teaching activity (the length, group size and subject will be dependent on the school) and a formal interview with the Head-teacher, Deputy Headteacher and 1 or 2 Governors. You may also be asked to do a presenta-tion, again on a subject of the school's choosing. However, remember you will be on show the whole day and it may well be that all staff feed back their thoughts on how you inter-acted in the staffroom, how many classes you visited etc. so make all of your interactions positive ones.

The key to being successful at interview is to be prepared. Dress smartly, this does not mean you have to wear a suit if this is not practical (which it really isn't for Primary Schools) but look like you've made an effort. Take everything you may possibly need for the teaching, even whiteboard pens, and if you plan on using ICT ring and check beforehand that it will be available and they have the software you are planning on using; however - have a back-up plan! You never know when ICT is going to break. Also, have someone look over your lesson and even try it out if you can.

It's not possible to second-guess what questions you will be asked in the interview but there are some things you can think about beforehand, and this page has a good selection: http://sites.google.com/site/tesfaqs/applications/interviews . Make sure you can talk about things you've written in your application, your educational ethos, why you want to work at that school, what you can bring to the role etc. If you're applying to a faith school you may also be asked how you will support this.

Finally, go home and wait for the phone to ring. Don't be disappointed if you don't get it and ALWAYS ask for feedback as it will help you improve next time. For more tips on job applica-tions and interviews try these two links:
http://issuu.com/dajbelshaw/docs/getthatjob?mode=a_p&wmode=0
http://sites.google.com/site/tesfaqs/applications

Good luck!

The NQT Year

The next step in your teaching career is your NQT (Newly Qualified Teacher) year. Below Oliver Quinlan shares his reflections on the differences between PGCE and NQT and what lies ahead!

Moving from PGCE to NQT by Oliver Quinlan

The PGCE year is spent with your eye constantly on one goal; passing and getting your QTS (Qualified Teacher Status). Once you have done that you will have your own job, your own class, the freedom to do things in the way you want to rather than just to pass observations. It is tempting to think that once you have passed you will know exactly what to do and be able to just get on with it, happily following your own routines. Hopefully you have come into teaching for the challenge, because whilst the PGCE course is a hard work, your NQT year is a whole different challenge.

There are bonuses of being a NQT: the relative freedom, the opportunity to get to know your pupils much better, and the chance to be a real part of a school community. However, there is also a whole new set of challenges, from being responsible for a whole year's worth of progress, to having to deal with the constant interruptions, changes of plan and organisational difficulties that you are often shielded from as a trainee.

One thing I can say is that whilst much of the difficulty of the PGCE was based on workload, paperwork and dealing with systems I did not agree with, I have been able to push myself even further this year for one single reason. Last year was about me satisfying people to give me a qualification, and hence many of its details were futile, although necessary for the end result. This year it was about real children and making a difference to their lives and hence, whilst it has at times been a struggle, it was always worth it.

So, what have been the challenges? The first one is unsurprisingly the transition from playing the PGCE game to actually being a class teacher. To me this is as much a culture shock as anything else. As a trainee you are used to thinking in weeks and days, one regular observation after another. You have to keep improving and you have to keep showing 'perfect' practice. Once you are in the job it changes, and is more about the long game. I have found this is less about having the stamina to keep it up full time, and more about the way priorities change and how this reflects in your practice.

For example I began this year wanting to be all singing all dancing, and jump straight in to the kind of exploratory, child led lessons I felt my choice of workplace had given me the remit to do. Big mistake. I began the year working at the edge of my ability in terms of pedagogy, and as a result it took me a long time to get the routines and respect in place that is needed if a class is going to go with you to the kind of learning culture I aim for. I was thinking in the short term, PGCE mindset when I should have been thinking about the long game.

My biggest piece of advice to new NQTs would be even if you are capable, don't try to be the all singing, all dancing teacher you want to be from the start, or even the one you were for your final observations on teaching practice. There is a temptation to think you have something to prove, especially if, like me, 150 people applied for your job. However, compared to the PGCE game you have a long time to prove these kinds of things. It is much more important to get routines and expectations in place even if, dare I say it, you are not doing great lessons in terms of teaching and learning. As a trainee I totally underestimated the amount of work my class teachers had done to get the class to a point where I could walk in there and start teaching them. Once I got into the long game mindset I did things differently. The rules had changed, and I found myself doing some things I had previously been very critical of other teachers for doing. I realised they weren't doing them because of the impact they had then, which can sometimes be questionable, but the impact they would have on the bigger picture, and the longer term. I also realised that every single little detail doesn't actually matter as much as you think it does when you are a naive trainee. Sometimes you don't do certain things in the best way possible, but as long as you always have in mind the long term goal of high quality learning it often doesn't matter. You really have to let some things go.

Despite the challenges, I have had lots of personal successes this year. Developing things that were points of weakness in my practice and turning them into strengths, building my confidence as a teacher massively, and coming up with some great lesson ideas I never would have thought of last year. However, the biggest success has to be the progression I have seen in the 31 children I have taught this year. The changes I have seen in their confidence, their work ethic, and their general attitude towards learning have been phenomenal, and I am very proud of the hard work they have all put in. There are, of course, many areas to continue to work on in my teaching, and that is the nature of the job, but I am pleased to have taken a class through a whole year and really made a difference to them.

To me, the NQT year is what you make of it. It could be an easier year than the PGCE if you choose to consolidate what you have learned, keep your head down and concentrate on doing what you did in your training. It can also be much harder if you really push yourself to make the most of your relative freedom and try things out. This is the start of your career, and the ultimate time to start showing people what kind of teacher you really want to be... Just make sure you are strategic about it, you are playing the game in the long term now.

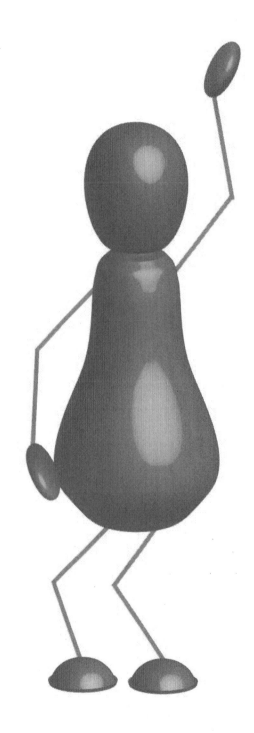

What we wished we'd known and our highlights.

What we wished we'd known before we started our training!

At the end of his NQT year Mark Howell published a blog post outlining 10 things he wishes he'd known before starting his PGCE. His post is below:-

Having now got out the other side of my first year proper I thought I would reflect on 10 things I wish I knew at the start of this. Many of them are things which people tried to tell me, but I always find I have to make my own mistakes in order to learn, never have been great at taking the advice of others. So in no particular order:

1) Not every lesson has to be perfect – Perhaps not true so much in PGCE as regular observations mean you have to be right on the money all the time. A mentor in my PGCE year told me that the way I planned lessons that year would be unsustainable on a full timetable. I was sure she was wrong; she was not. The hardest thing was accepting early on in my NQT year that sometimes you have to teach lessons knowing that you could plan a more engaging exciting version of it. But in order to have any kind of social life and keep a happy girlfriend you have to take nights off and you have to stop working, allowing some time before bed to chill.

2) Don't reinvent the wheel – Again I was told this by a Uni tutor almost 2 years ago and have only really realised lately how important this is. Throughout PGCE and the early part of NQT year I now realised I made extra work for myself by trying to jazz up lesson plans or school schemes of work that really were absolutely fine. I have learned that the process of improving SOWs needs to be an ongoing thing, do a couple a year rather than attacking all of them and trying to revolutionise geography overnight.

3) Enjoy the 'buzz' moments – As any teacher knows, the best part of this job is the buzz you get from time to time. Generally these come as a result of hard work and planning engaging lessons where great learning takes place. Initially I took these for granted but have begun to savour and enjoy these times more and more often. I also try to make sure I get one of these a week. Pick an exciting lesson coming up with a good class and spend some time creating something they can really get into. However, the best thing about the buzz moments is that often the best ones are not preconceived.

4) Save some enthusiasm – I well and truly burned out the last term of the year. I went into both years so far with maximum enthusiasm and I have had none left by the end. This may be easier said than done but I will try hard next year not to burn out.

5) Organise a trip – My best school related experiences came from going on the ski trip every year. I half heartedly suggested early on this year that I would like to do one and then just thought oh I will never be able to organise something like that. Thankfully a friend at school kicked me up the backside and we now have 35 kids coming to Italy with us in Feb. Yes, the organisation and paperwork is massive but it really is possible if you get a team around you. I have also had a chance to organise and lead 2 fieldtrips the last 2 years which again requires lots of time but is greatly rewarding.

6) It is normal to be so busy that lesson planning reduces in quality – Speaks for itself really. I went through a phase of feeling bad for my classes that lessons were not as good as I wanted for a while whilst coursework etc was going on. I realised again that there are times when this just happens.

7) You can make an impact – Before starting this I assumed that it would be years before I had any impact on the school I worked at. I was wrong. Being the first out and out geography teacher my school has EVER had has meant I have been able to exact big changes in the subject in 12 months. As a result next year we have an AS running for the first time ever with around 13 students. We also have 2 classes of geog running at GCSE next year, another first. Both of these steps forward have come about as a result of me changing the profile of the subject in the school and this is greatly rewarding.

8) Sometimes hoops just have to be jumped through – I made a big noise in PGCE (as did others on my course) about not just being box tickers. I have found this year sometimes you just have to do these paperwork, admin things and it's less hassle doing them than kicking against them.

9) The idea is not to be perfect yet – I spent a lot of time this year and last being disappointed that I was not the teacher I wanted to be. I realised around Easter that that is never going to happen so early. It was a real watershed the moment when I realised that I will be as good as I want to be one day and for now that will have to do.

10) Kids are forgiving (in general) – What I mean by this is you can make mistakes, or try new things in lessons and they may go wrong. Provided you don't do this all the time, the kids will forgive you and you can start again next lesson as if nothing ever happened. Inspired by this blog post the Twitterers were asked to share what they had wish they'd known before they started teaching - here is what they said!

Inspired by this blog post the Twitterers were asked to share what they had wish they'd known before they started teaching - here is a selection of what was said!

My friend wished she knew it wasn't so hard to get a teaching job - especially as a woman.
@Oxchris

Wish I'd known you don't have to appear omniscient. It's fine to admit ""I've never thought of that before"" or ""ooh I don't know""!"
@rantingteacher

I wish I'd known how to build relationships with parents. And understood what an emotional issue a child's education can be.
@bird42

#pgcetips- Our Highlights

We asked our Tweeters:-

What's your highlights from your teacher training?

Highlight of my PGCE was getting a buzz from teaching for the first time. Can't really beat the feeling of success in a classroom
@mark_howell101

Getting that job (10th interview in my case!)
@chris_1974

Organising and taking the children on a trip to the local park to look at   habitats. It was great!
@KnikiDavies

Getting involved in lots of drama and music. Meeting lots of like-minded people.
@KnikiDavies

Setting the school fire alarm off and evacuating the school - twice within 30 minutes... (best fuel praticle!)
@mrgpg

Best PGCE memory: all the children I made a difference
@oliverquinlan

The y7s leaving my room whispering that mine was their favourite subject during their first week :-)
@mandared

Being told you're getting it right either by well done from teach TY from kid or comment from parent.
@chris_1974

Being given my first teaching post by my 2nd placement school couldn't have asked for a bigger endorsement!
@STEMclubs

Final Top Tips!

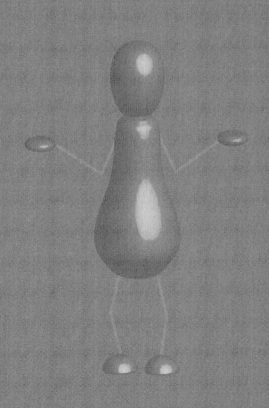

1. **Be prepared to learn lots!**

   During your teacher training you will learn lots - some of which you will expect to learn, and much more that you won't!

The things I know now that I didn't in September...

I thought it'd be good to provide a, hopefully humorous, reflection on the past term (my first on the PGCE, and therefore my first experience of teaching!)

So here goes with some of the things that I know/realise now that I didn't in September! (Take it as a given that there is a lot of practical/theory things learnt!)

Children say the funniest things- my favourite so far has got to be 'I'm not deaf eyed you know' from a year 3 boy in the middle of a argument.

The taught sections of a PGCE is very much like being in secondary school- and that I still don't like double maths!

That I would find myself doing gymnastics and dance in PE again!

That:- building bridges out of Sweets, having a tea-party with puppets, running around in a forest, dunking biscuits and potato printing, are all things I'd find myself doing in 'university'- and how much fun they were!

That you can use drama to teach practically anything- and that's it's a really powerful tool!

That the use of cake (coupled by the promise of being able to eat it if you work hard- not bribery honest!) works well with fractions.

That the way you teach calculations has changed a lot since I was at school- and that the 'new' way actually makes sense!

That I'd have received lots of 'job offers' already (Sadly (in a way!), they were all from the children in my class, so not 'real' ones- if only getting a job would be that easy!)

That children will love it if you turn their classroom into a crime scene- and not really realise they are doing maths- and that the headteacher won't hate you when she shows prospective parents round and the classroom door bears the sign 'Crime Scene enter with care'!!

That if you hand children a video camera you may not get it back that easily!

That I'd soon come to hate the words 'nice', 'and' and 'said'

That children love stickers, especially personalised ones with the teachers name.

That music can be an incredibly powerful tool in the classroom

That I could use fake snow and do some 'magic' when teaching absorbancy in science.

That you can teach art without being good at art.

That teaching assistants are some of the most important, useful and skilled people in the world (followed quickly by school receptionists!)

That Interactive Whiteboards are an invaluable tool for teachers (as long as you don't rely on them too much!)

That teaching is hard work (yes I knew that before i started!) but the enjoyment,fun, laughter and sense of achievement more than makes it worthwhile.

That having someone from university watching your lesson for the first time is one of the most nerve wrecking experiences ever!

That teaching has to be one of the best and most rewarding jobs in the word!!

2. Be Prepared to try new things

As Oliver Quinlan explained, being a trainee teacher is the perfect opportunity to experiment and try new things - make the most of it!

3. Be Professional

Make sure you appear professional at all times - both in dress and behaviour!

4. Embrace opportunities

Your PGCE year will be full of opportunities. Whether it's the chance to observe feedback to parents, accompany children on a residential trip, take an assembly or to go on an extra course or conference - embrace as many of them as you can.

5. Take a break

The PGCE year is hectic and busy - but make sure you take a break once in a while. Try to set aside some time each week where you are not doing anything to do with the course and give yourself some time off at weekends. Why not set up a series of 'treats' that you can look forward to throughout the course? You will perform better if you are rested!

6. Don't put things off

You will have so many deadlines on the PGCE and so many things to do. Make sure you don't put things off, as there often isn't time to catch up!

7. Don't reinvent the wheel

There are lots of great websites, lesson plans and resources out there - use them! Obviously don't use them without considering how they will fit your class, but use them as a base for your own planning. For a list of some see the next tip!

8. Technology is your friend

As a trainee teacher you have the perfect opportunity to embrace technology and use it to enhance your teaching. There are lots of great resources out there which can really enhance lessons and help you in your planning.

USEFUL ON-LINE RESOURCES

There are loads of fantastic websites out there which will be really useful to you as a teacher. I've collated just some of them below!

It's worthwhile creating a 'teacher' e-mail address (i.e. mrhandley@rocketmail.com) to use during your PGCE year - this way you can use this to sign up to all of the websites below, and your class won't see your 'real' e-mail address when you login at school!

Planning and General Resource Websites (mainly primary focused)

Teaching Ideas – www.teachingideas.co.uk – lots of excellent resources as well as a monthly 'theme' which is perfect for topic/thematic teaching! [LOGO]

Primary Resources – http://www.primaryresources.co.uk/ A goldmine of resources for all subjects!

TES Resources- www.tes.co.uk/resources
TES Resources hosts more than 46,000 free teaching resources for all subjects in Primary, Secondary and Special Needs

Teachers TV - www.teachers.tv Lots of great videos - for your professional development, lesson ideas and to use in class

Teachers Pet (UK) http://www.tpet.co.uk/#/home - lots of great downloadable resources, many flash based for use on the IWB.

Communication for all - http://www.communication4all.co.uk/HomePage.htm

Primary Languages - a must for anything to do with MFL in primary! http://www.primarylanguages.org.uk/home.aspx

Scholastic Child Education Plus - http://education.scholastic.co.uk/ - Child Education Plus is a great magazine that's published by Scholastic - but it's more than a magazine as it also gives you access to a bank of wonderful professionally produced resources and activities online which all look really great. There are lots of free things on the website; subscription to the magazine and site does cost but is well worth it!(It's not much though and there are some super student deals if you are a PGCE student.)

Teachit Primary - lots of free resources, but you do have to pay for full access. http://www.teachitprimary.co.uk/

Teaching Search - http://www.teachingsearch.co.uk/ searches across a lot of the main resource sites.

Tools for the Classroom

Jog the web – http://www.jogtheweb.com/ It basically allows you to collate numerous websites together into a 'jog' which is accessed by 1 link. It has lots of potential uses in sharing sites with children etc.

Wordle and Kin - www.wordle.net For those who don't know, Wordle lets you produce wordclouds which visually represent a piece of text and show you which words have been used most etc. In some schools Wordle won't work (due to a common firewall issue) but ABCya have another alternative and Tagexdo is a newer, more advanced version.

Wallwisher – www.wallwisher.com This site has been used in some great ways by teachers and Wallwisher is best described as an online 'sticky note board' - people can visit a 'wall' you set up and leave notes which are instantly viewable by everyone else.

Piclits – www.piclits.com This is a website I only discovered a few days ago and it links quite well into the thoughts I've been having regarding the power of images. It's worth visiting and having a play around with it, but basically you pick a image from their image bank (some great images) and then try to create a sentence/phrase to describe the image or convey a message etc - there are 2 options - one which provides lists of verbs, nouns, adjectives etc which have been chosen with that particular picture in mind for you to simply drag, drop and arrange, and the other is 'freestyle' which allows you to enter any text you wish. Some of the examples in the gallery look great and I think this could have some really great uses in the classroom - especially when looking at description etc in English or as a slightly different approach to symbolism in RE/PSHCE etc.

Voki - www.voki.com Voki is great! It allows you to create speaking characters (avatars) which you can voice with either a voice recording or through an advanced text-speech engine which works in lots of languages, making it an ideal tool to use in MFL lessons. I do warn you - creating Vokis can be addictive - especially if you are like me and take great care (too much

care!) in how my vokis look

Memiary - http://edu.memiary.com/ This is a great little tool that allows you to enter '5 things we've learned today...' and store them. It's really simple to use and the new education version is even better! It's really great to use as a review at the end of each day and children love doing it! I'm a big believer in reviewing learning and this is a great way to do it! Sign up to the EDU version and convert your account to a teacher account and you can have much more control!

Purplemash – www.purplemash.com This is a brand new website by the wonderful people at 2simple. It's a great online suite of tools, including some of 2simple's 'best' products - including 2design and make (which allows you to design your own 3d models via nets), 2 sequence (really fun audio sequencer) and 2Publish - there are also some great templates to use as 'APPtivities' (for instance, at the moment, just as 2 examples, there is an election poster and a news story about an animal escaping from a zoo). As it's online it also means the 2simple team can update it etc! There is a 'free range' mash version which has lots of activities etc available for free and they also do a "gourmet mash' version which costs £500 a year for a school which provides access to even more, including online versions of lots of 2simple software.

BrainpopUK - www.brainpop.co.uk I have to admit it, I love Tim and Moby! For those of you who don't know who I'm talking about(!) Tim and Moby are the 2 wonderful characters who explain lots of things in really clever, simple and entertaining short movies to children. They are, in my opinion, simply the best at explaining things and my placement classes LOVE them. They have films for practically every subject and are always adding more. Tim and Moby do a very good job at introducing themselves in this video and you can access the featured video each week for free. Subscription does cost money (but they aren't too expensive for a school to buy) and they offer a 1 month free trial anyway!

Primarypad - www.primarypad.net Again, one that lots of people will know about already - but for those who don't, it's a great collaborative writing tool - it basically allows multiple users to edit one document at once, in real time and see what other people are typing as they type! I've used it before and have blogged in more depth about it here and about a different use of it here - but I think it's great and a really valuable tool which has so many uses! Primarypad has now moved across to a 6month trial basis and then to continue using the pro features you need to purchase access for your school.

Primary Games arena - http://primarygamesarena.com/ has lots of games, all classified, which could be great to use in class/on the IWB etc...

Wordpress.com – http://wordpress.com A great blogging platform - why not investigate setting up a class blog in your placement school? (check with your school first!)

Storybird – www.storybird.com - Storybird is basically a collaborative storytelling/writing tool. Two (or more) people can create a Storybird in a round robin fashion by writing their own text and inserting pictures - there are some great illustrations provided for children to use and it's as simple as dragging and dropping. The finished Storybirds I've seen all look really impressive! As well as writing it collaboratively it can also be used to write individually and create individual Storybirds. Finished work can be shared online (or kept private) - I think this could be a really great tool to use and it could provide a different motivation for creative writing etc...

Animoto – http://animoto.com/education   This is perhaps one of my favourite online tools at the moment. Animoto makes really impressive videos from images (and shorts bursts of videos) you upload. It basically analyses the images and the audio you choose and automatically 'professionally' cuts a video. The results are stunning - it's a slideshow without being a slideshow! I've used it to celebrate work and projects etc... The free education version is well worth signing up for!

Google Docs - http://docs.google.com Google docs now includes lots of real-time collaboration features which can be used in similar ways to Primarypad.

And 3 websites to help you organize yourself!

Drop Box - www.dropbox.com or http://bit.ly/pgcedrop not a site you'd probably find need to use with your children but one which can save you a lot of hassle! Dropbox is an online storage/synchronisation service. You can put items into your dropbox and they are automatically available on any other computer you choose to install the Dropbox software on (which basically creates a virtual 'drive') or any computer you have access to (via the web). It could make it easier to transfer files between home and school etc! Sign up via http://bit.ly/pgce-drop and you'll get an extra 250mb of storage space!

Evernote - www.evernote.com A great website for organizing all the information and links you come across.

Delicous - http://delicious.com/ A great website which allows you to create a 'portable' bookmark list - essential for organising all the links you have and ensuring you have the links in school!

9. Be prepared for any eventuality

Schools are dynamic and ever changing places and children are certainly not predictable. Make sure you are prepared for any eventuality - especially when a lesson involves a particular resource or ICT! Most importantly, be prepared to be flexible!

10.   Read Blogs

There are so many teachers out there that blog, all of which give interesting viewpoints, opinions and resources.

There are lots of great teaching blogs out there, but here are a few to get you started!

Classroom Tales/ Tales from a NQT - The blog of Tim Handley, the editor of this book! www.classroomtales.com @tomhenzley

Year Six Teacher (now a year 3 teacher!) http://yearsixteacher.blogspot.com/ (@yearsix-teacher)

Digitial Teacher http://www.digital-teacher.co.uk/ (@xannov)

Adventures in Learning http://ebd35.wordpress.com/ (@ebd35)

Teaching News - Latest education news, links and resources http://www.teachingnews.co.uk/ (@teachingideas)

Primary Pete- http://primarypete.net/ (@primarypete_)

Edte.ch – the blog of @tombarret on Twitter- http://edte.ch/blog/ (@tombarrett)

Doug Belshaw - http://dougbelshaw.com/blog/ (@dajbelshaw)

Classroom TM - http://www.classroomtm.co.uk/ (@mrlockyer)

Ollie Bray- http://olliebray.typepad.com/ (@olliebray)

Kevin Mulryne - http://www.mulryne.com/ (@kevinmulryne)

What will Julia Do next? - a light hearted blog about teaching + more- http://jfb57.wordpress.com/   @jfb57 (@TheHeadsOffice)

Jenny Harvey: @relativism blog's - http://relativism-studentponderings.blogspot.com/ and http://jenny-ict.blogspot.com

Oliver Quinlan - http://www.oliverquinlan.co.uk (@oliverquinlan)

Chickensaltash- http://chickensaltash.edublogs.org/

ICTSteps - http://www.ictsteps.com/ (@kvnmcl)

AskSir - the blog of @DeputyMitchell on Twitter - http://mrmitchell.heathfieldcps.net/ (@DeputyMitchell)

Bill Lord - http://lordlit.wordpress.com/

Geographical Association Blogs- http://www.geography.org.uk/resources/geographyblogs/

Lisibo - http://lisibo.co.uk/ (@lisibo)

Primary MFL- http://primarymfl.ning.com/

Kerry Turner- http://www.kerryjturner.com/

Chrisrat – Chris is a sales director at Scholastic UK- http://chrisrat.com/blog/

The Langwitch Chronicles - http://www.helenabutterfield.net/

TILT- http://tilttv.blogspot.com/

From Dawn till Dusk - http://hallyd.edublogs.org/ (@dawnhallybone)

Ian Addison - http://ianaddison.net/ (@ianaddison)

Andy McLaughlin - http://ajmclaughlin.wordpress.com/

Chris Mayoh - http://chrismayoh.blogspot.com/ (@chrismayoh) - Educational technology and the home of the 'Innovating with iPods' series

Scitt Science - the blog for @dannynic's primary PGCE science students http://www.scittscience.co.uk (also incorporating Scittipedia)

The Whiteboard Blog - the IWB advice blog of @dannynic http://www.whiteboardblog.co.uk

Mark Howell - http://markhowell101.wordpress.com/ (@mark_howell101)

E-learning Experiences - www.nstoneit.com/ (@nstone)

Kristian Still - http://www.kristianstill.co.uk (@KristianStill)

11.Reflect Reflect Reflect

reflecting on yours and others'
practice is vital on the PGCE.
Make sure you reflect on your
experiences. One great way to
help you reflect (often without
realising it) is to start up a
blog!

12.Join Twitter

All of the #pgcetips in this guide have come from the wonderful world of Twitter. There is a vibrant, dynamic and incredibly useful network of education professionals on Twitter - why not join Twitter and join in the conversation and benefit from all this expertise. Twitter is a great way to build up your personal learning network (PLN) - why not start by following the tweeters who contributed to this guide - I'm sure they would be more than happy to follow you back and help you get your PLN started!
See http://bit.ly/pgcetip1 and http://bit.ly/pgcetip2 for more infoormation on getting started!

13.Have fun + Enjoy

Above all make sure you enjoy your PGCE year. It is a fantastic year that will be full of many high points and wonderful experiences. You are joining one of the best professions there is.

All the best this year. Make the most of your holidays and make sure you enjoy being in a classroom as often as possible @mark_howell101

Enjoy have fun make sure to laugh lots both with your students and colleagues @nstone

Have a great year and see you on Twitter!

Tim and the rest of the #pgcetips contributors!

Welcome to the best job in the world. @christoclifford

Printed in Great Britain
by Amazon.co.uk, Ltd.,
Marston Gate.